31 states have now passed laws allowing the concealed carrying of firearms. Citizens and police have a duty to teach the safe and responsible use of these weapons!

This handy little book contains everything a novice gun owner needs to know to start learning the basics of competent and safe pistol use, as well as the essentials of using a gun in a potentially violent confrontation with a criminal.

It is also an ideal textbook for state courses required to obtain a concealed-carry permit.

While there are many excellent books on handguns, marksmanship and self defense, all are designed for those who want to be expert in those subjects. There is no other book which addresses the specific concerns of someone who simply wants to carry a concealed firearm safely and responsibly — until now.

One of this book's primary goals is teaching how to <u>avoid</u> discharging your firearm in the first place — stopping aggressive criminal behavior without having to shoot someone.

The Practical Pistol Manual brings all your concerns together — safety, competent shooting, and how to deal with violent behavior — in one concise and affordable book.

The Practical Pistol Manual

How to Use a Handgun for Self-Defense

by Bill Clede

Jameson Books Inc • Ottawa, Illinois

ISBN: 0–915463–74–1

Photos by author unless otherwise credited.

Jameson Books, Inc.
722 Columbus Street
Ottawa, Illinois 61350
815-434-7905
FAX: 815-434-7907
email: 72557.3635@compuserve.com

Jameson Books are available at special discounts for bulk purchases. Please write the publisher for information.

Jameson Books' titles are distributed to the book trade by LPC Group, 1436 West Randolph Street, Chicago, IL 60607. Bookstores should call 800-243-0138.

Individuals wishing to buy copies by mail order, please call 800-426-1357.

Manufactured in the United States of America.

4   3   2   1   98   99   00   01

Contents

A Word of Caution

Arming yourself carries with it the obligation to know not only *how* to use your gun but also *when* to use it. This is a decision only you can make as you face threatening behavior. You can be sure you will be second-guessed by the police officer responding to your call, and possibly also by a judge in court — civil or criminal. "Justification" depends on the laws of your state and the actions of your assailant.

The use of a gun is considered deadly force, even though studies show that four out of five persons shot by police do not die. You must be justified in using deadly force. The proper application of law, of forceful techniques, or of tools must be justified under the law as it applies in your jurisdiction. Alleged misapplication or misuse of any law, technique, or tool — whether discussed here or not — can make you vulnerable to a lawsuit or to criminal charges.

The purpose of this book is to make you aware of the "safe and responsible use of firearms," according to some states' definitions of required training. It is *not* to make you a champion marksman.

The publisher, consultants, and author accept no liability of any sort for any personal injury or property damage that might result from the use or misuse of any information, techniques, or applications presented or implied in this book.

Acknowledgments

I often say, "I'm not so smart myself, but I have a lot of intelligent friends." The use of firearms has been my lifelong study but I could not have written this book without the help of those friends. I owe a debt of gratitude to all who are quoted herein. *They* are the experts.

Special thanks are due to Lt. Herb Burnham (Ret.), former head of the Connecticut State Police Weapons Unit, and to Lt. Col. Matthew F. Tyszka, Jr., Commanding Officer of Administrative Services, responsible for our state's CCW training program. These men read the manuscript as it developed and offered constructive criticism.

My thanks to the demonstrators who posed for photographs. They showed you the proper techniques because they are experienced gun handlers: Sgt. Tom LePore and his wife Nicole; Lt. Joel Kent (Ret.), Windsor (CT) Police Department; Lt. Steve Knibloe (Ret.), East Windsor (CT) Police Department; Officer Bruce T. Howard (Ret.), New Britain (CT) Police Department; and Ed Dalenta and Andy Pappas (Ret.), of the Connecticut State Probation Department.

Introduction

Police officers spend weeks learning about their sidearms. They engage in exercises to practice their skills. They must be able to recognize a threatening situation in an instant, and to react properly — before they become another "Officers Killed" statistic. Their gun skills are so important that they spend at least a week in basic firearms training, and then they reinforce their skills with in-service training several times a year for the rest of their careers.

So, why are *you* interested in carrying a gun? Police officers wear their guns as defensive weapons — and that should be your reason as well.

Most states have laws requiring a permit for anyone who wishes to carry concealed weapons (CCW). In 1995 alone, 10 states enacted such laws. At this writing, 26 states require applicants for these permits to complete a training course. I serve on the Connecticut State Police firearms advisory committee which designs the training my state requires. The many fine books on gun handling, marksmanship, and confrontational behavior are directed at specialists in those subjects. I perceived a need for a book intended to help the people who simply want to qualify for their CCW permits and to conduct themselves responsibly when they carry their pistols.

This is that book.

It addresses the concerns that arise when you decide to arm yourself. It is not *Everything You Wanted to Know about Handguns but Were Afraid to Ask*. Instead, it offers an understanding of the basics. If you learn something here that sparks a deeper interest, ask your instructor where you can learn more, or consult your local police department and ask to speak with the firearms instructor.

This book is thorough enough to be used in formal training in some states and for self-training in others. First, it discusses the capability for self-defense. In Part I, it addresses the areas of study that are essential if you are going to carry a concealed weapon. In Part II, it discusses matters you may not have considered before you decided to arm yourself. I have included here, without apology, several police stories. After all, most of my instructing experience has been training police officers. This is also the group for which statistics are most available. And finally — police are people, too. What differentiates a police officer from you is the level of training he or she must complete before pinning on that badge and taking the oath.

Never get the idea that you're some kind of superhero just because you're armed. Police are trained to apprehend criminals. You are not. Your reason for wearing a gun is to protect yourself or a loved one from death or grievous bodily harm.

"Self" Means YOU

A few times in my otherwise low-key life someone has pushed my hot button. I could feel the blood rush into my head, and I knew my face flushed. One more second and I could have launched like the space shuttle.

But that wouldn't have been very professional.

Self-control

A study of the health risks posed by anger was released in 1994. One of the authors, Dr. James Muller of Deaconess Hospital in Boston, explained that when a person reaches the fist-clenching, teeth-gritting level of anger, his or her chances of suffering a heart attack double during the next two hours. Adrenalin surges, veins constrict, and blood clots more quickly; the response is similar to the physical reaction to overexertion. For some people, such anger is almost a daily occurrence.

"Such people need stress-reduction training," Muller said. "They need to address their response to stress and learn to control it."

Although trainers have long known that police officers must control themselves before they can control a situation, the focus of training has always been on controlling others. Clearly, a police officer who flies off the handle easily will generate, rather than solve, problems, and the same is true for other citizens. *A hothead should not carry a gun.*

"The public expects police to be professionals and not fall into the provocation trap," says Chief Ron Patla of the Burlington, Wisconsin, Police Department. "We are the ones with the skills to remain in emotional control and not go ballistic." That must also hold true for you when you carry a gun.

You may encounter a belligerent or extremely annoying person who tries your patience. There've been times I was sorely tempted to take on some obnoxious character. But it's far better to remain self-controlled and use your verbal skills to de-escalate a situation. It's also far easier than explaining the obnoxious one's injuries in a court of law.

The police course on self-discipline and emotional control teaches trainees how our minds interpret events and attach meaning to them, and how that feeling produces a behavioral response.

Dr. Tom Miller, a psychologist, points out that our behavioral responses may be overreactions. He explains the irrational thinking that gives rise to such overreaction and suggests ways to alter the thinking process. By changing our thinking, we can change our behavior.

Consider these examples:

- A husband brings his wife a bouquet of flowers. Is he expressing his love and appreciation? Is he easing his guilt about something he should not have done? Is he smoothing the way for some bad news? Whatever the case, her reaction will be determined by what she thinks he is doing. That is, if she thinks the flowers are an expression of love, she'll be delighted — even if they're really an expression of guilt. On the other hand, if she thinks they're an expression of guilt, she'll be suspicious.

- You get a sudden sharp abdominal pain. Maybe you're suffering from gas after a spicy meal. Maybe your peptic ulcer is acting up. Maybe your appendix is inflamed. Will you take an antacid, call your doctor, or go to the emergency room? What you do will depend on what you think is happening.

- Many people are afraid of flying. All of them share the same phobia, but some refuse to fly while others manage to overcome the fear. Of those who fly, some use air safety statistics to convince themselves that the risk is minimal; some believe that there are lies, damned lies, and statistics, but decide that they are brave enough to risk being airborne.

In fact, overreactions — indeed, all reactions — are learned behaviors and can be unlearned and replaced with responses that will better serve our purposes.

"Count to ten before you react" has always been good advice, but it is especially so when you are armed. You can do serious damage to an assailant, so you must keep your cool and do nothing you cannot justify to a responding police officer and/or to a presiding judge.

This book isn't a technical treatise on ballistics, but let's clear up one thing right at the start:

There's no such thing as a magic bullet.

The first gun I carried was a Smith & Wesson .38 M&P model with a four-inch barrel. For those too young to remember, that's a .38 S&W Special, and it was a big improvement over the once-popular .38 S&W cartridge. I'm as caught up in this "arms race" as the next instructor. For the officer on the street, I consider the .40 S&W high-capacity pistol to be the minimum suitable carry gun. It worries me to see so many in plain clothes wear the "puny" .380 auto. Nevertheless, now that I've retired from the department, the gun I wear most often is that same .380 auto.

At one time I convincingly argued that, based on ballistic tables, the .380 is almost comparable to the .38 Special. The 9mm is better, but it doesn't match the .357 Magnum. The 9mm's advantage is its larger-capacity magazine: in a pinch, I'd rather have 17 not-quite-so-powerful cartridges available than 6 more powerful ones. These preferences come from personal experience of various kinds, such as shooting falling plates with various guns. "Falling plates" is a target event using steel disks that fall over when they're properly hit by your bullet. When I visited International Practical Shooting Confederation (IPSC) champion Tom Campbell some years ago, I put the piece I was wearing at the time — a 9mm Glock 17

— through its paces. I also brought along a pair of .380 autos that I'd bought years earlier for my wife and my elderly father. Those guns needed the exercise.

When the .380 hit the plate, there was a thud and a wobble before it slowly toppled. With the Glock, there was only a *clang* before the plate disappeared from view. But ballistic charts and falling plates aren't the whole story. I'm going to repeat one thing endlessly in this book: *The only reason you fire is to stop an aggressor's felonious assault.* Now, if I shoot someone on the street, I don't want a wounded attacker to kill me then slowly expire from loss of blood. I want the most effective cartridge I can find. Still, it's an axiom among police that, "I'd rather be missed by a .45 than hit by a .22." My baptism in the murder business was a gas station robbery. The robber had herded the attendant into the men's room and blithely pumped a couple of shots into his chest — from a .22 pistol. The kid was just as dead as if he'd been hit by a .45.

Bullets do vary, and whole books have been written about their relative stopping power. Modern "controlled expansion bullets" are designed to penetrate their target several inches, then upset themselves and stop. They impart maximum kinetic energy to the target and will not over-penetrate and pass through to wound an innocent bystander. I'll take any advantage I can get, but sexy bullet design runs a distant second when it comes to doing the job of self-defense.

Lab analysis may show that a bullet will penetrate 14 inches into ballistic gelatin and create a greater wound cavity that its competitor. Fine. Some experts slaughter animals to evaluate the performance of a bullet, then they write articles for gun magazines. That's fine, too. But none of it means a thing in terms of the challenges that face you on the street unless you remember:

You must hit what you're aiming at.

Some training targets are constructed with a circle at the top and then a four-inch stripe down the middle. Why? Because only a hit to an attacker's central nervous system guarantees instant incapacitation.

Look at that answer again: It includes absolutely nothing about bullet design or caliber. Bullet *placement* is the key to stopping a felonious assault. With a properly placed bullet, you can stop an attacker almost as quickly with a .380 as you can with a .45.

For a long time, I regret to report, police bullets hit their targets only some 17 percent of the time. "Real situations being what they are," explains instructor Robert M. Irwin (who is also a justice-court bailiff in Clark County, Nevada), "you aren't attacked by a docile person. The one thing *you* can control is bullet placement. Put a bullet — any bullet — into the brain or spinal cord and you get instant incapacitation."

Irwin isn't entirely correct here. There are *two* things you can control. The other one is *yourself*. In Irwin's words, "It's not the maker of the sword, but the courage and skill of the swordsman that will win the day. The 'magic bullet' is *you*."

Part I: *The Course*

States that require gun owners to undergo training specify the topics that training must cover. This part of the Manual includes those required subjects and may be used as the text for a handgun training course.

— 1 —
Safety Is Your Responsibility

You have decided to arm yourself. You have visited a local dealer and chosen your handgun. If you are not already licensed to carry, you are in the process of qualifying for a CCW permit. In all this you are exercising your constitutional right, but rights include responsibilities. Think of your gun as a power tool. You wouldn't dream of operating an electric drill or a chain saw without knowing how to use it safely. Because of its lethal potential, your pistol must be treated with commensurate respect.

Safety must be your first concern.

Safety rules

1. **T**reat every gun as if it were loaded.

   If you keep a gun for protection, you must keep it ready for instant use — especially if you are wearing it away from home. In the house, even if you store your gun empty, always act as if it were loaded.

2. **A**lways point the muzzle in a safe direction.

   My mother taught me it was impolite to point my finger and it's more than rude to point a gun

1

at anyone — in spite of what you see in movies or on television. If someone walks in front of you when you are holding a firearm, raise it or lower it so that it is never pointed at a person.

3. **L**eave your finger off the trigger until you're ready to shoot.

An unintentional discharge is at least embarrassing and at worst catastrophic. Firearms are manufactured with built-in safety mechanisms. Indeed, a modern, properly functioning pistol virtually cannot fire unless someone pulls the trigger. Nevertheless, mechanical devices can wear out, break, or malfunction, so don't depend on your gun's safety catch.

4. **K**now what is beyond your target.

The hunter has to identify her target to be sure it is legal game. If you are using a pistol for self-defense, you've already identified your target — but what's behind that target? What if a lunatic is shooting at you while standing in front of a crowded playground? Can you risk killing someone's child?

You can readily recognize a person who is well-trained in the use of firearms. The gun is made safe as soon as she picks it up, and she never points it at anyone or anything she doesn't intend to shoot. Anyone who waves a gun around, points it "playfully," or is careless with it is ignorant, a danger to herself and others.

TALK

Note that the rules above form the acronym TALK. The more you learn about responsible gun use, the more you'll realize that the gun is only one of your self-defense tools. Studies by Dr. Gary Kleck, a criminologist at Florida State University, show that firearms are *involved* in some 2.5 million self-defense situations each year — but in only a tiny fraction of these instances is the gun *actually fired.*

Talking can protect you, warn any friends who are with you, and give your assailant time to reconsider. For example, one cold night a friend of mine encountered someone in the parking lot where he had left his car. The person approached threateningly, so my friend opened his coat and said, "You wouldn't want to do anything that would force me to blow your face off." He didn't even have to touch his gun to ward off the assault.

Wearing a gun safely

If you wear a gun on the street, you want to feel comfortable, you don't want to drop it, and you do want it handy if it's needed. These are the essential considerations when you're deciding how to carry your gun. I once wore a four-inch-barrel

Notice that the belt slide holster for the pistol (left) covers the trigger guard and provides retention. The pancake holster for the revolver may be put on the belt with a forward tilt or straight up.

revolver in a pancake-style holster on a normal dress belt. With each step I took, the pistol gave me a kidney punch. The problem was not with the gun or holster, but with the belt. When I replaced it with the two-inch belt the holster was made for, the gun rode snugly and securely on my hip.

In addition to choosing the gun, the holster, and the belt, women have the option of buying a handbag designed for carrying a gun. Either sex can wear a fanny pack made to hold a gun.

This book can't begin to discuss and describe the wide variety of handguns and holsters on the market. Consult with a

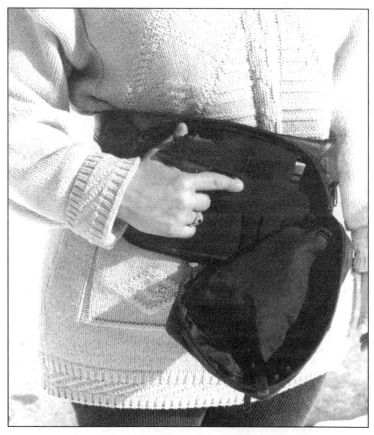

The fanny pack is an alternative for men or women. Pulling one tab strips top and side zippers exposing the gun for the draw.

knowledgeable friend or your gun dealer. Based on your particular needs, a revolver may be a better choice for you than a semiautomatic pistol — or vice versa. I grew up using a revolver, that four-inch-barrel Smith & Wesson Military and Police Model in a .38 Special. When I retired from my last department, my duty gun was an S&W Model 66, .357 Magnum revolver, so my off-duty gun was a .38 Special S&W Chiefs Special, with a pair of speedloaders to fit it — the same basic design as the gun I normally wore.

Your choice of holster depends on a number of factors. A shoulder holster is fine if you customarily wear a coat or jacket — so it's not as good in hot weather. There are shoulder holsters that hold the gun vertical, horizontal, or upside down. Inside-the-pants holsters can be worn on your hip or in the small of your back. Holsters can be worn on your ankle, or in your pocket. There's even a belly-band type to wear under a shirt.

A wide variety of pistols and revolvers may be used for concealed carry provided they are properly rigged to wear comfortably.

You might consider the option of a handbag or briefcase that's made to hide a handgun but keep it readily accessible. Your local gun dealer can probably advise you on this decision.

Keep it simple. I prefer a right-hip holster that holds the gun snugly against your body just behind your strong side. Years of wearing a police duty belt conditioned me to instinctively reach for my right hip. A friend of mine left the police department and went into Executive Protection. He changed to a front cross-draw holster so he could draw through a buttoned overcoat. He practiced with it for four months before he felt confident with it.

A business suit, of course, is tailored to your normal body. When you strap on a gun rig, something isn't going to look right. Whenever I buy a new suit, I put on my gun rig before I have it fitted. Whatever you decide about your gun, your holster, and your belt, remember that all three are important. Together, they can save your life, so think carefully about whether you want to save some money by buying an inferior product.

If you are going where a gun is inappropriate, do not carry one. If you're headed for a night on the town, you shouldn't be wearing a loaded gun. You know that alcohol and gasoline don't mix — well, neither do alcohol and gunpowder. Some states prohibit carrying a gun — even with a permit — in bars, schools, and some government buildings.

Which reminds me of another concern. At one time, I worked at a radio station. Every workday morning for three years I drove to a parking garage, then walked four blocks to the studios at 4:30 a.m. At a reunion a few years later, the subject of carrying a gun came up in conversation, and I said, "I wore a gun all the time."

Another station alumnus said, "I never knew that."

"That," I told him, "is because I know how to wear a gun."

Keeping it concealed

Eventually wearing a gun can become second nature to you, but in the meantime you can be very self-conscious — which makes it hard to keep your gun concealed. John O'Reilly is a retired vice officer who now works in executive security, and he is trained to spot people who are armed. "People carrying guns," he observes, "pat them constantly. If they wear a shoulder holster, their arms hang away from their bodies on that side." He also mentioned other dead giveaways: clothes don't hang right; one side of the shirt collar pulled lower than the other, the buttons not quite aligning; and exposing the firearm — if it is worn on the hip — by bending over to pick something up.

In the early 1950s, I was working my way through college as a police officer, and I was a shooter on the rifle team. Once we traveled to New York City for an intercollegiate competition, and we stayed in a dorm at City College of New York. The neighborhood wasn't really bad, but we were from out of town, and we'd heard stories. Besides, I was required to wear my badge and my gun. Anyway, three of us had gone to a movie on Broadway, not far from CCNY. We were walking back to the dorm about 9:30 that evening. Street lights lit the area as if it were daytime. We turned up a side street about a block from the college and saw four seedy-looking characters across the street, coming from the other direction. They crossed to our side of the street and came toward us in a line, blocking the sidewalk.

"Uh-oh," said one of my teammates.

I unbuttoned my blazer and unconsciously flipped the coat-tail (it's called "clearing your coat," and it's an automatic reflex when you think you may have to draw your gun). To this day I have no idea whether those guys had malicious intent toward us or not. But they recognized my move and promptly crossed back to the other side of the street.

Nevertheless, the point of wearing a concealed gun is to keep it concealed. That way, if you are accosted, you have the element of surprise working for you. You lose the advantage if you show your gun. What's more, you can get your carry permit revoked if you go around "flashing" your pistol and bragging that you are armed. The gun, after all, is only one tool you use in self-defense. And it's not the most important one.

Storing a gun safely

When burglars break into a house, the first place they look for a gun is in the bedside stand. If you have children, they

It's important that your kids understand the power potential of that "little" gun. When they see a water-filled oil can or milk jug explode, they get the picture.

will quickly learn that's where you keep your gun. Think about it. Is the bedside stand a good place to keep a gun? Of course not. Your dresser drawer isn't a place that will protect the gun from dust and dirt, either.

My kids were taken to the range as soon as they could hold a gun. They had an opportunity to satisfy their curiosity and to shoot at plastic milk jugs filled with water to see the damage a gun can do. They learned early to treat a gun with respect. But they had friends who were not so familiar with guns. In your home, you must safeguard not only your own kids, but also their visitors. Even if you have no children, can you guarantee that none will ever come into your house? Probably not.

If you have several guns, the best place to store them is in a gun safe. If you have only one handgun, it's best to store it in a pistol pouch. A number of products on the market will store your one pistol safely, keep it away from curious children, and yet make it accessible for you if you need it. Your dealer can help you choose what you need.

Some states, such as Connecticut, have passed laws making gunowners responsible for the negligent storage of a firearm.

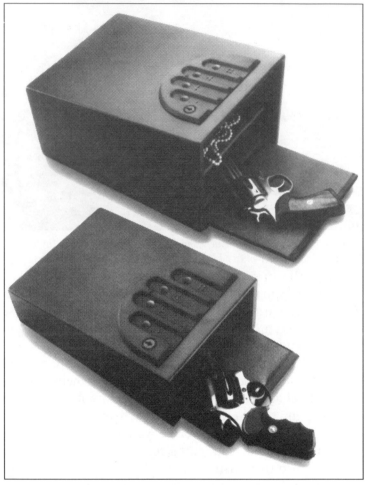

These quick access one-gun boxes are the MiniVault from Gun Vault Inc. They offer both a key and a finger pad combination lock so you can access the loaded gun inside in a hurry. The larger model can hold other valuables as well.

— 2 —
The Gun and Its Care

The many parts of a handgun can be grouped according to their major functions.

Gun parts

- The **receiver**, sometimes called the frame, is the base to which the other parts are affixed. It usually includes both the **grip**, by which you hold the gun, and the **action parts**, by which the gun functions.

- The **barrel** is attached rigidly to the frame of a revolver. On a semi-automatic pistol, the barrel fits inside the **slide**.

Ammunition parts

Ammunition design is an entire study in itself. For our purposes all you really need to know is enough to allow you to select the best cartridge for your use. A cartridge consists of four major parts:

- The **cartridge case** is the brass cylinder that contains the other components.

- The **primer** is the "spark plug" in the center of the base in a center-fire cartridge or in the heel (rim) of the case in a rimfire cartridge.

- The **powder** is the combustible material that burns when ignited by the flash from the primer. It generates the gases that push the bullet through the barrel.

- The **bullet** is the lead or jacketed projectile in the front of the cartridge case. There are, of course, several types of bullets.

Handgun ammunition is designed for specific purposes. A **target load**, for example, is intended for accuracy and will cut a clean hole in target paper. Usually, it contains a modest powder charge so the shooter will not be exhausted after a sixty-shot training course. A **hunting load** is intended to perform at higher velocities, so it is "hotter." It pushes the bullet faster and is designed to expand inside a game animal.

Any bullet enters its target, then expands like a mushroom so that its speed slows rapidly. This efficiently transfers the bullet's kinetic energy to its target. A "controlled expansion" bullet may look like a hollow point, have a partial metal jacket

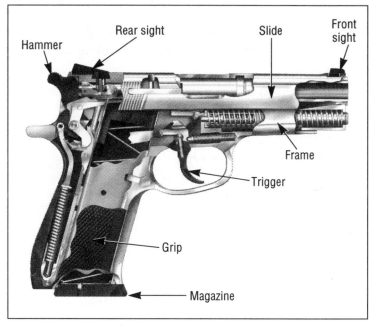

The Smith & Wesson semiautomatic pistol is typical of the DA/SA (double action/single action) pistols. The first shot is double action. Then the act of firing cycles the slide (the top part that moves) to eject the spent case and pick up a fresh cartridge from the magazine that holds additional cartridges in the grip. This leaves the gun cocked and loaded so your next shot is single action. Some semi-autos are designed to be double action, cocking the hammer and causing it to fall on the cartridge after a complete pull of the trigger. (Illustration provided by Smith & Wesson)

with a soft lead tip, or show construction that makes it easier for it to upset in a controlled manner. These bullets are *not* "dum dums".

Loading and unloading safely

When people ask me, "Is your gun loaded?" I reply, "Of course it is. It's not much good without ammunition." Remember the first safety rule: *A gun is always loaded.* So it must be unloaded before you clean it. Unloading procedures vary depending on the type of handgun you use, but these instructions will hold true in any case. (The instructions presume you are right-handed.) *Always point the gun in a safe direction.*

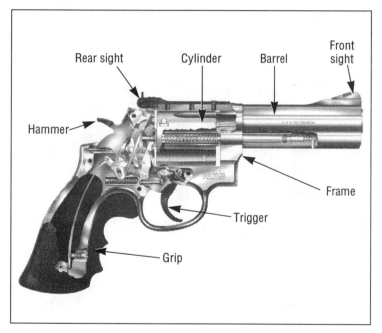

This Smith & Wesson 686 "double action" revolver can be fired by simply pulling the trigger. This rotates the cylinder so the next cartridge is in place and cocks and the hammer at the same time. By cocking the hammer with your thumb, "you can fire it single action". This also turns the cylinder, and firing the "cocked" revolver requires much less trigger pressure. Shooting the gun single action results in better accuracy, but it takes valuable extra time in a crisis situation.
(Illustration provided by Smith & Wesson)

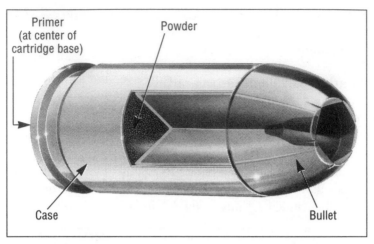

A 9mm pistol cartridge is sectioned to show the four component parts: case, primer, powder, and bullet. (Illustration courtesy of Remington Arms.)

Cartridges from left are a .380 ACP JHP, 9 mm Nyclad HP, .38 Special Nyclad HP, .38 Special lead HP, .357 Magnum AP, .357 Magnum SP, .45 Colt lead, and 45 ACP FMJ.

1. If you use a modern *revolver*, hold it in your left hand, release the cylinder with your right thumb, and push it open with the fingers of your left hand. (With the cylinder open, the gun cannot fire.) Drop the cartridges onto the table and put them away.

   For a modern *pistol*, release and remove the magazine. There may still be a round in the chamber, so draw the slide back and lock it open. (With the slide locked open, the gun cannot fire.) Let the ejected cartridge fall out, then slip your little finger into the chamber to be sure it is empty. Put the ejected cartridge away.

2. To load the *revolver,* follow the unloading procedure to open the cylinder. Then insert cartridges into the open cylinder and close it firmly with your left hand. **Never slam or flip the cylinder shut.** To load the *pistol,* first be sure the chamber is empty: Pull the slide back and let it go forward. Then insert the loaded magazine. Depending on the design of your pistol, you may be required to engage a safety or use a de-cocking lever. Always read and understand the manufacturer's manual before you attempt to disassemble or use a new firearm.

My preferred "carry mode" for a single action semiautomatic with an exposed hammer (e.g., the Colt 1911A) is: loaded magazine but empty chamber, slide closed, and hammer down. It takes only a second to cycle the slide as you draw the pistol. My Glock, on the other hand, is designed to be carried with the chamber loaded. So I cycle the slide to strip a cartridge from the magazine, then remove the magazine and insert another cartridge to replace it.

Field stripping for cleaning

You need not disassemble a revolver to clean it. You can reach everything you need to reach with the cylinder open. The pistol, however, is a bit less tolerant of dirt and grime. With the slide locked open, you can reach the barrel, but you have to remove the slide to clean the rails. Different pistols have different modes of assembly, but they all require you to remove, turn, or hold down some piece of the hardware so the slide can move forward. (At this point, be careful to contain the recoil spring so you don't lose it.) Now you can remove the barrel from the slide. That's as much as you need to disassemble a pistol for cleaning. To reassemble the pistol, simply reverse the procedure.

Because there are so many varieties of pistols, it would be impossible in this limited space to describe the assembly of each one. If the manual that came with your gun does not answer your questions clearly, talk to your gun dealer or a firearms instructor.

How to clean your gun

Opinions vary on the subject of cleaning your handgun. I clean inside the gun barrel every time I use it. You can simply

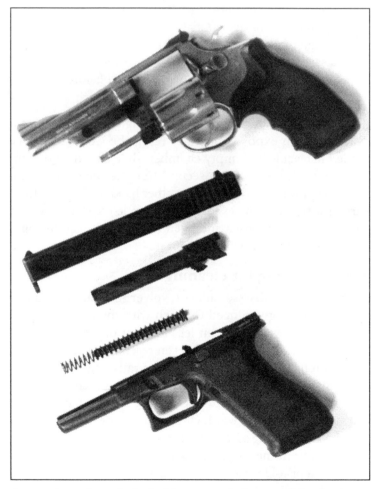

Opening the revolver cylinder (top) lets you reach what you need to clean. A pistol should be field stripped only down to these major components for cleaning.

moisten a patch (cloth designed for cleaning guns) with powder solvent and run it through the bore. Repeat with new patches until one comes out clean. An aerosol can of compressed air will blow dust and lint out of the barrel. More thorough cleaning is probably not necessary unless you've dropped the gun into sand or mud. Then you must field strip it and clean each part — at which time you can give the barrel a complete cleaning.

When you clean a **revolver**, pay particular attention to the surfaces that are engaged by the cylinder pin to lock it. Powder residue can build up on the face of the cylinder, on the chamber end of the barrel, and under the top strap. When you clean a **pistol**, take special care with the channels in the slide and with the frame along which the slide moves when the gun is fired. By taking the barrel out of the slide, you can clean it meticulously, inside and out. You want to keep the magazine clean because that's what enables the pistol to function. If you damage a magazine in any way, replace it with a new one.

It's best to use oils, solvents, and patches intended for use with firearms.

Before you reassemble your gun, oil it wherever metal rubs against metal. Always remember, though, that gun oil is like castor oil. A little is good (perhaps a drop of oil on a given spot), but a lot is definitely *not* better. Excess oil attracts dust and will eventually gum up the works of your gun. What's more, some newer oils and solvents are penetrants — they can actually seep into the cartridge case and render the primer inert. Therefore, *always wipe excess oil off the firing pin area and keep it away from the cartridges.* Finally, always use fresh ammunition. You can keep the older stuff and use it for practice.

— 3 —
How to Shoot

You may not be planning to compete in Olympic shooting events, but you need to achieve some level of marksmanship if you are to defend yourself by hitting an assailant some distance away. But how far away is an attacker likely to be?

Statistics show that most police-involved shootings occur at a distance of five to seven feet (yes — *feet*) and the vast majority at a distance of under seven yards (21 feet). Also, most shootings take place in dim light or near-darkness. So it doesn't take Olympic-caliber marksmanship to hit your target, but it does require mastery of *technique*. We're going to discuss two specific shooting techniques — one for use in close-quarter situations and another that applies when the threat is farther away and you have more time to respond. First, however, we need to cover your grip and your stance.

Grip

You know that it's important to hold the saw correctly when you are cutting wood. And you know that a golfer's grip can determine the accuracy of his drive. Grip is equally important in shooting, because a proper grip minimizes muscle strain and is less tiring.

- Hold your right hand up (or your left, if it's the stronger) with your thumb and fingers extended.
- With your left hand, place the gun into the web of your right hand (the soft part between your thumb and first finger). If you use a revolver, the top of your hand should be at the top of the grip. If you use a pistol, the back of the grip flares near the top to help keep your hand in proper position.

19

- Now wrap your finger around the gun, keeping the barrel of the gun in line with your forearm (just as when you point your index finger, it's in a line with your forearm).
- Keep your wrist locked and rigid. If your wrist moves, the gun wavers, and you cannot shoot accurately.
- Practice this proper grip so that you are comfortable with it.

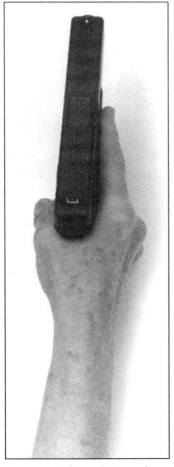

A proper grip keeps the gun in line with your forearm.

Stance

When you are threatened, you undergo stress. Your body reacts accordingly. Adrenalin begins pumping through your system, you square your body to the source of the threat, you focus directly on it, your muscles contract convulsively, and you instinctively drop to a crouch.

Colonel Rex Applegate, a world-renowned authority on combat shooting, developed close-quarter shooting techniques first for the Office of Strategic Services (OSS) during World War II. He contends that much of today's pistol training works against the body's natural reactions to stress. Instead, Applegate suggests, "Why not use these natural reactions in a shooting technique that is easy to learn and easy to retain?"

In close-quarter situations, Applegate recommends *point shooting.*

- Pick a spot on the wall and face it.
- With your strong arm angled downward about 45 degrees, point your index finger. Keep your elbow and wrist locked.
- Now, focusing on that spot, raise your arm from the shoulder like a pump handle and bring your finger into your line of sight. Surprise! You're pointing at the spot you selected, right?

One-hand technique

In point shooting, when you've drawn the gun and don't have to fire right away, drop your arm down about 45 degrees. Nicole LePore shows that you can see without obstruction, and if you need to shoot...

It takes little time to raise your arm like a pump handle and bring it to bear.

Gripping your gun properly, repeat the steps of Applegate's point shooting. With practice, you won't need to sight your gun — you may not have time to sight it anyway. On television you see police officers using the two-hand technique. That's fine if you have time, according to Applegate, but at short distances the one hand reaction is quicker and more natural.

Two-hand technique.

Picture the way a boxer stands facing his opponent. He's turned a little off full front with his strong side slightly away.

His weak arm is in a protective position while his strong arm is ready to strike. Police officers assume a similar stance (they call it the "interview" stance) when they are talking with someone. The officer may be taking notes or whatever, but her gun side is turned slightly away from the other person. If she needs the gun, she can draw it quickly.

The boxer's stance is quicker and requires the least movement when you start from the "interview" position.

I like this boxer's stance for two-hand shooting. You hold the gun in your strong hand with your arm extended straight.

Then you bring your weak hand up to the gun, keeping that elbow slightly bent, and wrap those fingers around those of your strong hand. This helps support the gun and, by pushing slightly with the strong hand and pulling slightly with the weak one, you give the gun a more stable platform.

Some prefer the isosceles stance: your arms form a triangle and you face the target straight on. Bend the knees to keep yourself flexible.

You may find it more natural to face your target squarely, feet slightly apart, knees slightly bent, and bring the gun up to eye level. This is called the isosceles stance because it forms an isosceles triangle.

The basics

In addition to the basic concerns of grip and stance, other considerations can improve your shooting even though you will not consciously apply them when shooting in self-defense.

Breath control

Your whole body moves as you breathe. Hold the gun out in front of you and watch it. See it move with each breath you take. In shooting, breath control simply means that you stop breathing as you pull the trigger.

Sighting

In target shooting, it is critical to line up the front sight with the notch in the rear sight. This is called *sight alignment.* Then you line that up with the target bull's-eye so that it visually sits on top of the front sight. This is called the *sight picture.* If the front and rear sights are off by just a fraction of an inch, that distance will multiply as the bullet travels to the target. You will miss by a mile. Remember: a gun in good condition is accurate — it puts the bullet where the sight is aiming. You have to practice to become as accurate as your pistol.

When sighting, the alignment of the front sight post in the notch of the rear sight is critical. Notice that this front sight is slightly to the left. That error is multiplied by the distance to the target.

Trigger control

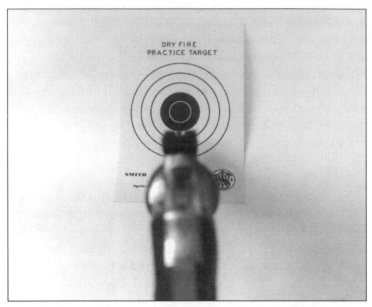

If you focus on the target, your sights are fuzzy. That's fine when point shooting at close range, but in sighted fire, this off-alignment will result in the bullet hitting far to the left of the bullseye.

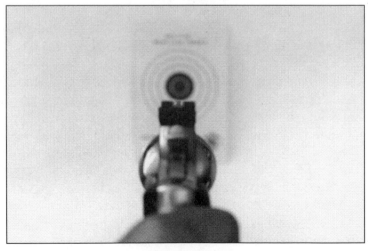

With the sights perfectly aligned, you need not see a sharp target to put a bullet into the bullseye.

Trigger control simply means the slow, steady increase of pressure on the trigger until the gun fires. At first, try not to know when that will happen. If you anticipate the gunshot, you are likely to flinch and knock the sights out of alignment.

True, you may want to pull the trigger quickly in self-defense, but if you practice this fundamental motion slowly at first, you will develop good trigger habits.

Follow through

Golfers and tennis players complete their swings after they hit their balls. Likewise, you want to continue aiming your gun after you've fired. In terms of accuracy, this will help you avoid bad habits. In terms of self-defense, it keeps your attention focused on the threat so you will know whether another shot is required.

Getting the gun into play

By now, you should have decided how you will wear your gun. Let's assume you wear it as I wear mine — in a snug right-hip holster on a suitable belt. With practice, you can develop a fluid motion, swooping your hand to the gun butt, gripping it securely, and keeping your trigger finger extended along the frame. You then lift the gun from the holster and bring it in front of you in a smooth arm motion. Only then should you bring your weak hand up and use both hands to raise the gun to eye level.

Always grip your gun (whether one-handed or two-handed) with the trigger finger straight along the frame and your wrist locked. Only when you are ready to shoot should your finger go into the trigger guard. I've timed the difference between finger inside and finger outside the trigger guard, and the difference is negligible. By keeping your trigger finger *outside,* you'll avoid firing prematurely.

One of Colonel Applegate's commandments is, "Thou shalt not shove thy handgun." "Shoving," or throwing, your gun is like throwing a baseball. When you throw you add a flip of the wrist to increase the speed of the ball. But when you shoot, your wrist *must* be locked — you can't point a gun or even your finger unless your wrist is rigid. If you hold a handgun high and "throw" it toward the threat, your shot is likely to hit the ground before it reaches your assailant.

In Tucson, Arizona, in 1992 Daniel Bennett was working in his pizzeria when two armed men entered and shot him in the chest. He drew his newly acquired Glock and returned fire, but the gun failed to function after the first round, and the attackers fired five more shots into him. Bennett sued the gun manufacturer, the distributor and the dealer on the grounds

The draw begins with getting a good grip on the gun while it's in your holster, finger alongside the frame, as Tom LePore demonstrates.

that the firearm was defective. He contended that they failed to warn him that the gun could malfunction, and failed to instruct him in its operation. His suit contended these failures led to his injuries.

At the trial, it was revealed that Bennett had bought the gun and a box of ammo, had learned to load the magazine, had put it into the pistol, and had chambered a round. And that was it. He did have the presence of mind to draw his gun in self-defense, but *he had never learned how to shoot it!*

Lift the gun from the holster and bring it toward the front, finger still alongside the frame. Now your left hand can begin to move up.

Apparently, he "limp-wristed" the self-loading pistol so that it failed to chamber the second cartridge. Gun writer Jeff Smith calls this "the classic freshman flunk."

Glock attorneys were able to teach the jury enough basic physics to explain how a recoil-operated firearm works, and the jury decided that Bennett should have learned how to use his defense gun. After all, when you buy a car, the dealer doesn't include a drivers' ed course. The buyer is responsible for using his purchase safely and responsibly.

When the gun is safely past all parts of your body, then the left hand fingers wrap around your strong hand grip. Notice that Tom steps toward the dumpster.

How to Shoot 31

Now, let's suppose you are gripping the gun properly. Your assailant's movements require you to move around. What's the safest way to do that? First, remember that your adrenalin is already flowing. What if a family member suddenly comes on the scene and startles you? *Keep the gun pointed in a safe direction* — usually downward at a 45 degree angle — and *keep your finger off the trigger.*

Keeping your finger off the trigger will keep you from firing inadvertently, and keeping the muzzle pointed down at a 45 degree angle will prevent a tragic accident even if you do fire.

Bring the gun up to your eye level. Do NOT duck your head down to the gun. At this point, your finger may enter the trigger guard, if you're going to shoot. Also notice that Tom squatted down to take advantage of the dumpster's cover potential.

Finally, *never move sideways by crossing one leg over the other.* You don't want to stumble or trip with a loaded gun in your hand, so if you must move, sidle.

Reflexive shooting

Up to this point, we've been dealing with purposeful training on the shooting range. You may not expect to need this information in real life, but you will. If you understand not only *what* to do with your gun and how to do it, but also *why* it's done that way, you are more likely to get into good habits. When you know how a proper grip and stance *feel* and how a sight picture *looks,* you won't need to think about any of that when you confront a threat.

A military artillery piece is accurate at long range because it rests on a solid **gun mount**. In a variation of this solid base, a quail hunter mounts his shotgun against his shoulder. For pistol shooters, the gun mount consists of all the elements we've been discussing; stance, grip, draw, sighting, breath and trigger control, and follow through. Like an experienced golfer who can tell by the feel of a good drive that the ball is headed straight for the green, the practiced shooter knows the feel of a shot that will hit the bull's-eye.

In an instructor class I completed some time ago, I saw a practical illustration of this point. The instructor was Jerry Lane of Offshoots Training Institute of Kennesaw, Georgia. He taught us the proper way to mount a shotgun, then kept us practicing that for half a day, always urging us to shoot faster. Then he took us to a darkened shooting range with barely enough light to see the targets — and definitely not enough to see the sights. Nevertheless, after that practice session, everyone in the class was able to hit the targets every time.

This, by the way, is one reason I rarely carry a snub-nose revolver. I like a four-inch barrel that's visible in my peripheral vision. My subconscious mind knows where the gun is pointing.

"Point shooting" describes what you do when you've practiced enough to be a comfortable and confident shooter. All the details you learned on the target range become second nature to you. At short range, you can focus on the actual threat rather than on the gunsights. Almost subconsciously your eyes will line up the sights and your finger will pull the trigger.

Even in minimal light, point shooting lets you know when your "gun mount" feels right. Then remember that you *never move by crossing leg over leg.* If you face two threats, address one and then pivot on the balls of your feet to confront the other.

Also, keep in mind that shooting on the target range and shooting under duress are not the same. You may be able to hit the target with every shot at practice, but when you're threatened — when your heart thuds in your chest and your breathing accelerates and you have to react rapidly — you'll be grateful for what you learned about point shooting.

Maintaining your skills

If you used to ride a bicycle everywhere but you haven't been on one for years, you don't expect to hop on a bike and be as sharp as you were as a kid. The same is true of shooting and of any other motor skill. Fortunately, though, some serious practice will refresh your muscle memory. If your shooting skills are rusty, go back to the target range and you'll find yourself regaining your expertise with less effort than it took to learn the skill originally.

The best way to keep yourself up to par is to find a local gun or sportsman's club (some even specialize in pistol shooting). Even if the club offers only target practice, it's worth your time and effort. You may need remedial training only in the basics. If possible, find a club with a certified pistol instructor who has experience with new shooters.

— 4 —
Practical Concerns

Wearing a gun responsibly involves more than just knowing how to shoot well. When you carry a concealed handgun, you have a capability of which the aggressor is unaware. Therefore, you need to be more judicious in your behavior than if you were unarmed. A friend of mine (who, by the way, is the closest thing to a gunslinger you're likely to meet nowadays) always carries a $20 bill wrapped around a book of matches. If he's accosted on the street, he offers the "gentleman" the $20 in the hope that he will take it and go away. It's worth $20 to this man to avoid using his gun.

So after you've learned how to handle your gun safely and shoot it accurately, your next concern is finding ways of never *having* to use it. You learn to avoid dangerous situations and to become more amicable. A wise man once said, "An armed society is a polite society."

At home

Your first concern around your home is probably burglary. Of course, that's not personally threatening because it's a property crime, right? Wrong! One Bureau of Justice Statistics study reports that, "Three-fifths of all rapes, three-fifths of all robberies and about one-third of all aggravated and simple assaults are committed by burglars."

You may believe, along with many other people, that a burglar is probably a neighborhood kid after your stereo. Actually, in 30 per cent of the incidents in which a burglar was confronted by a household member, a violent crime was committed. Most burglars are professionals.

Have you ever locked yourself out of your house? How hard was it to get in? My neighbor locked herself out once and came to me for help. Rather than call her son, who lived in a nearby town, to come with a spare key, I used a small screwdriver and a sliver of plastic to open her door in about 30 seconds. Her locks were old and the tumblers were worn, so it was easy. A skillful burglar can manage a newer lock with nothing more than a credit card. All my door locks are deadbolts, but even these require a sturdy door jam or a burglar can simply kick the door in.

The fact that more burglaries occur in summer than in winter, doesn't mean burglars dislike cold weather. It means that people are likely to leave doors and windows open for ventilation in hot weather, and most screen doors have only flimsy latches.

Many homeowners take pride in their landscaping, but a clump of greenery outside a window offers a burglar a convenient hiding place while he works on his entry. Porch and street lights help to eliminate shadows, and I've added dual flood lights at one corner of my house to light my driveway and the rear apron of the garage. Motion detector switches on outdoor lights will cause them to come on when anyone or anything approaches — even a raccoon bent on raiding your garbage can.

Some burglars watch homes to be sure the owners are away when they break in. Others, however, don't care. They may actually ring your doorbell and ask to come in and use your phone. When a motorist had car trouble outside my house one evening. I did let him in to call for help. I wondered why he looked so nervous — until I noticed my 100-pound dog standing quietly but menacingly in the hallway, baring his teeth in a snarl.

Yes, dogs can help deter burglars. In fact, a small but noisy animal may be more discouraging than an affable Doberman — but don't depend too heavily on your pet. Some burglars regularly carry treats to help them make friends with your watchdog! One convicted burglar, asked what would scare him away from a home he intended to rob, replied, "*Two* Dobermans, and a homeowner who looks like she knows how to use the gun in her hand."

All this is by way of suggesting that you evaluate your residence. Pretend you're a burglar and look for houses that would be an easy target. Can you spot some dead giveaways that a house is empty? Outside lights left on all day? A lawn that needs mowing? Piled up newspapers or uncollected mail? On the other hand, which do you think a burglar would shy away from? A house with a loudly barking dog? A house displaying alarm system signs? A house with nosy next door neighbors? A house that shows signs of the comings and goings of several residents?

Once inside, burglars will check all the standard hiding places: bedroom dresser drawers, bathroom cabinets and counters, even freezers. They may concentrate on small, easy-to-carry items like cash and jewelry. If they have a car hidden nearby, they'll grab bigger merchandise — TVs, VCRs and guns. Sometimes they'll hide the loot and pick it up later.

Where could a burglar lurk around your house? Keep your shrubbery trimmed. Are your doors and windows secure? Can you see through the front door to find out who is ringing the bell? If you can't, have a peephole installed.

On the street

You'd be amazed at how oblivious people can be when they walk down the street. They're often as unaware of their surroundings as they would be if they were in their own living rooms. A thief can snatch a woman's purse and catch her completely by surprise. What if she's carrying a gun in that purse?

Once in a while you may have to venture into an area where you know you'll be vulnerable. How can you minimize that vulnerability?

- Be aware of what is going on around you. Observe other people and watch for places where a thief could be waiting.
- Look confident — walk briskly and keep your head up.

- Avoid walking alone at night, if possible.
- Try never to park in an unlighted area.
- Detour to avoid groups hanging around building entrances, alleyways, or street corners.
- If you suspect you're being followed, head for people and lights.
- If someone in a car approaches as you're walking, turn abruptly and run back the other direction.
- When you're driving, keep the doors locked and windows rolled up.

Being aware allows you time to react to a threat. Your gun won't do you any good if you reach for it too late.

Controlling a threatening situation

All right, suppose you have to go into a hazardous area of the city. No one is available to accompany you. So now you are confronted by a person who intends to rob, rape, or assault you. (Or, if you prefer, imagine that you are confronting a burglar in your home.)

The first step in controlling the situation is to remain confident that you can. Stay calm. Slow your breathing, and be ready to speak clearly and firmly. Your voice, remember, is your most powerful weapon. Your words and your manner can let this aggressor know that you won't be an easy victim. *Your gun is always your last resort.* Dr. Kleck's study showed that 99 times out of 100, self-defense required only the *presence* of a gun, not the firing of it.

Self-defense is best achieved by avoiding a confrontation, and — if that's not possible — by avoiding using your gun. In effect, you are *willing* to use your gun, but you don't *want* to use it. You simply want to stop the aggressor and control the confrontation.

Parent-Adult-Child

In 1964, Dr. Eric Berne wrote *Games People Play.* The theory behind this book is that every person has three distinct selves, or "ego states": parent, adult, and child. No matter how old we become, we never entirely lose the child in us. That can be a positive factor. It allows us to have fun, to retain a sense of joy and wonder. The parent in us reminds us — as parents do — to be careful, to remember our obligations, etc. And that is a good thing, too.

But under stress, the parent and child in us tend to supersede the adult, so we have to consciously call on the rational adult self.

If we're startled or frightened, we may find ourselves sounding like parents: "Stop that!" "You shouldn't do that!" That approach will often bring out the child in the other person: "I can if I want to!" This dialogue is almost certain to produce conflict. The better approach, as Dr. Berne illustrated, is adult-to-adult. This is the basis for my friend's habit of carrying that $20 bill. In effect, he's saying, "Look, let's make a deal. You get $20. I get left alone." Any statement that doesn't force the other person to become defensive, to feel a need to prove something, or to forfeit self-respect keeps the dialogue on an adult level.

Signs of emotional disturbance.

Watch for signs that indicate your own emotional state and/or that of your aggressor. Clenching fists, rapid breathing, sweating, a reddened face, screaming, ominous silence, crying, trembling, stammering, a fixed stare, or tantrum-like behavior are signs of stress. When you recognize any of these signs in yourself, calm down. When you see them in someone else, be very cautious — the person could become violent.

De-escalation techniques.

Dr. George Thompson, author of *Verbal Judo,* suggests a system for neutralizing negative behavior or even redirecting it into positive channels. In order to defuse a conflict, you have to know what caused it. Who is involved in the conflict? Is he or she playing to an audience? What are the barriers to effective communication?

Keep your words on the adult level — that is, don't express feelings, opinions or value judgments. With that in mind, follow Dr. Thompson's LEAPS system:

1. **Listen.** Often, when we are in a conflict, we try to forcefully express our own views. That's natural but it doesn't help. Unless you face immediate threat of bodily harm, listen to your aggressor. Find out what he's thinking.
2. **Empathize.** Put yourself in your aggressor's place, and do it out loud. Let him know you're trying to see the situation from his viewpoint.
3. **Ask.** Inquire about how he feels, what he intends to do, what he would do "if." This tends to ease the tension because the aggressor will focus his attention on answering your questions. Often, he is glad to have the chance to speak his mind.
4. **Paraphrase.** Repeat what he is telling you in your own words. This is a neutralizing tool. It lets you interrupt without creating resentment or resistance. It makes the other person listen, creates/reinforces empathy, and produces a feeling of "fair play" — after all, you've listened and tried to understand. Now the aggressor will listen to you. He almost has to, after you listened to him.
5. **Summarize.** When you summarize what's been said — adult to adult — you move the situation toward closure. "So you're out of work and you really need this money. Okay, take it and walk away." Let the verbal give-and-take between you and your aggressor end in as much of a "win-win" resolution as possible.

Unfortunately, many confrontations on the street are instigated by an aggressive male who believes he has found an easy female victim (because women are supposedly disinclined to fight). A woman who has prepared for such an encounter by carrying a gun must decide *where* to carry it.

Purse snatching is such a common crime that in many large cities victims are urged to phone in the report when they get home. Calling in from the scene of the crime serves no purpose, because by the time an officer can respond the perpetrator will be long gone. And even if he's found, most victims cannot identify him based on the split second glimpse they had. So it's important to carry your handbag properly — especially if it contains your gun. Cradle your purse in your arm, close to your body, even if its strap is securely over your shoulder.

Imagine that you are standing at a crowded bus stop. A stranger sidles up close and tries to fondle you or reach into your purse. Your gun is no help to you here. First of all, the aggressor is too close to allow you to draw your gun. Second, he has not indicated any deadly threat. Third, to fire a gun in a crowd would be utterly irresponsible. Remember your most powerful weapon, *your voice*. Use it. **Loudly!** Virtually any offender will slink away from the crowd around you.

Now imagine the crowd has dispersed. You're waiting at a corner for the light to change so you can cross the street. Suddenly, there's an arm around your neck and a threatening voice in your ear. Turn your head so your chin is in the crook of the attacker's elbow. This will protect your airway. Then SCREAM! You can simultaneously jab him in the solar plexus with your elbow and knock the wind out of him. Or your fist can swoop down between his legs and give him a more serious pain to think about. A ball point pen jabbed into the back of his hand may force him to let go of you.

What about your gun? It's an alternative only when you have the space to use it safely. Anyone close enough to grab you is too close for you to shoot. You must first do something to divert the attacker and then get far enough away so that you can go for your gun.

After you've forestalled the attack, you may be questioned by a police officer. Where is your pistol permit? It should be with your ID and your driver's license. Tell the officer you are armed and that you have a permit. Keep your hands in full view. *Don't* carry the gun in your glove compartment. If you're stopped for a traffic violation and reach for your registration or

When someone gets his arms around you, a pen from your pocket will encourage him to remove his hands.

insurance information, the gun may slide into view. Suddenly you're staring down the muzzle of the officer's gun. The police do not like surprises.

If an intruder gets into your home, he has already demonstrated felonious intent but he may or may not threaten violence. Gather family members in one room (determine in advance where this "safe room" will be), lock the door, and call the police. Tell the dispatcher where you think the burglar is and what precautions you have taken. If you are armed, tell the dispatcher so that responding officers won't be caught off guard. Stay calm. Answer the dispatcher's questions. Stay on the phone until police arrive. Do *not* try to locate the burglar and hold him at gunpoint till the police arrive. Police are trained for the risky business of "clearing the house." Let them do their job.

After retreating to your safe room, call police while one person watches the stairs or hallway. Notice the guardian keeps his body hidden behind something — anything.

Elements of a deadly threat

Whether you're at home or on the street, you shoot to stop a felonious assault *only if the attacker may cause death or grievous bodily injury to you or a family member.* Your actions will be judged later by police and possibly in a courtroom. You must be able to explain your behavior. The fact that you were *frightened* does not mean that you were actually *threatened* and does not legally justify shooting. Legal justification requires the presence of three elements:

- **Jeopardy.** The aggressor's actions must put you or someone else in danger.
- **Ability.** The aggressor must have the ability to harm you or someone else.
- **Means.** The aggressor must have the means to carry out his threat.

Suppose you're walking down the street and you see a man coming toward you carrying a baseball bat. He has the *means* to harm you, but he's certainly not a threat at this point. As he comes near enough to reach you with the bat, he has the *ability* to harm you, but he's still not a threat. Then he raises the bat in both hands and starts swinging it at you. Now you are in *jeopardy,* threatened, and may be legally justified in responding.

After the fact

Any time a civilian uses deadly force — or even displays a firearm — responding police officers will be on edge. Let's say you are holding a would-be attacker at gunpoint when police arrive. What do they see? Two citizens — both unknown to them —one of whom is armed. Promptly obey any orders they give, and then identify yourself. Do whatever they ask, and let them sort out the situation.

Police investigating any incident are required to determine exactly what happened, so answer their questions. However, they will also be investigating the possibility of criminal action on *your* part. After you've identified yourself and told the police what happened, don't make a statement until you've consulted an attorney, and have your counsel present when you actually give a formal statement.

You may have been forced to take drastic action to stop an aggressor, and your actions may have been entirely necessary and fully justified. Nevertheless, if you have taken someone's life, that deed may have a profound effect on you. You'll question what you did: Could you have handled the situation differently? Could you have avoided it altogether? That reaction is natural. Many police officers have been devastated by post-shooting trauma. So go ahead and review your actions. If you followed the suggestions in this book, you used your gun only as a last resort. The aggressor made the "shooting decision." You simply defended yourself.

— 5 —
Familiarity with Your State's Law

All fifty states and many branches of the federal government have their own laws and interpretations on the *use of force*. Obviously, we cannot cover all that material here; but when you decide to carry a gun, you become responsible for familiarizing yourself with the laws of your state. Because some of the principles underlying these laws are almost universal, we will discuss situations which call for you to make a judgment. This will be essentially a moral, rather than a legal, discussion. I am not a lawyer, and this is not legal advice.

The basic premise of all that follows here is that you may use deadly force (in this case, a gun) to stop or prevent the use of deadly force against yourself or another person. Since the U.S. Supreme Court's 1985 ruling in the case of *Tennessee v. Garner*, not even police officers may shoot a fleeing felon. (In actual fact, they are sometimes permitted to, but only under very limited circumstances. These exceptions are of no concern to you: Your job is simply to protect yourself, not to apprehend criminals.)

The following is an excerpt from one of five separate laws dealing with this subject in my state:

> "a person is justified in using reasonable physical force upon another person to defend himself or a third person from what he reasonably believes to be the use or imminent use of physical force, and he may use such degree of force which he reasonably believes to be necessary for such purpose; except that deadly physical force may not be used unless

the actor reasonably believes that such other person is (1) using or about to use deadly physical force, or (2) inflicting or about to inflict great bodily harm."

This law codifies your right to act in self-defense, but it specifies that you may use *only as much force as is necessary to save yourself* (or another person). If someone harasses you by calling you names, punching him in the mouth would constitute excessive force and would not be "reasonable." Clearly, if an attack on you is strictly verbal, your gun must stay in its holster.

Scenarios

In the previous chapter, we talked about recognizing the elements that constitute a threat and about controlling a confrontation. Now we'll consider some scenarios in which you will need to make a decision.

You are walking along a dark sidewalk toward your parked car. A voice from a doorway shouts, "You'd better get the hell away from this neighborhood before you get yourself killed!"
Do you shoot?
No. This sounds to me more like good advice than a threat. I'd reply, "Thanks for the tip. I'm on my way!"

A man is standing in your way as you approach your car. He says, "Got a dollar for a cup of coffee?"
Do you shoot?
No. There is no threat, overt or implied. You would not be justified in shooting.

A man is blocking your way to the car. He shows you the gun in his hand and says, "Give me all your money."
Do you shoot?

Consider the circumstances. His gun is in his hand and yours is still in its holster. You can't possibly draw and fire before he shoots you. Think about my gunfighter friend and his $20 bill. Maybe giving him your money is better than shooting or being shot and dealing with those consequences — especially if your children are with you. If your cash satisfies the robber, you can walk away. If not, you still have choices: You can try to divert your assailant's attention so you can draw your gun. The fact that you are armed may scare him away. But so far you are justified only in showing your gun. Until the robber gives you reason to believe your own life or someone else's life is in imminent danger, you may not shoot.

◊   ◊   ◊   ◊   ◊   ◊   ◊

In the scenario above, the robber sees your gun, realizes you're not an easy victim, and runs away. **Do you shoot?**
No. You may be justified in drawing your gun to ward off the perceived threat, but when the robber runs, the threat is ended.

The next scenarios present more complicated "plots," and suggest how situations may be interpreted in more than one way. The point to keep in focus is that your "window of justification" exists only while you are in danger.

You return home to find a burglar looting your house. He sees you and runs toward the back door. **Do you shoot?**
Probably not. Some states allow shooting to prevent a felon's escape, but the general rule is "no." You shoot only to stop an aggressor's felonious assault on yourself or another person.

Instead of fleeing, the burglar drops the loot and lunges at you. **Do you shoot?**

*Probably. If you're sure he's lunging **at you** and not toward the open door behind you. If he is displaying a weapon, your justification for shooting is increased.*

You find the burglar holding his sack of loot and standing over your spouse, who is lying in a pool of blood.
Do you shoot?
No — not based on the information given here. You are certainly justified in holding the intruder at gun-point until police arrive. If he's still holding a weapon and turns it on you, that constitutes a threat, and then the answer is Yes.

You are walking past a park late at night. You see a woman tied to a tree and a man tearing off her clothes.
Do you shoot?
Not right away. Start with your most powerful weapon, your voice. Be ready to draw your gun if it's needed, then challenge the man —from a safe distance. If he tries to attack you, you may be justified in shooting. If he runs away, you call the police and try to help the victim. But if he and the woman explain that they are spicing up their marriage . . . wish them a nice evening and go home.

As you pass a convenience store, you look into the lighted interior and see an armed robbery in progress.
Do you draw your gun and go in to stop it?
No. Charging into a situation like this can get the clerk killed. Call the police, then find a defensible position from which to watch the store. Observe cars, license plates, and the appearance of the robbers. You aren't a police officer, but you can be a good witness.

◊ ◊ ◊ ◊ ◊ ◊ ◊

You've gotten into your car and rolled down your window for air. Before you can drive away, an attacker sticks a knife through the window and orders you to get out of the car.

Do you shoot?

*That depends. Clearly **jeopardy, ability,** and **means** are present But can you slam the car into gear and stomp on the gas to get away? If so, you can be sure a prosecutor will point this out in court. On the other hand, if your car is boxed in in some way, you may have no choice but to shoot.*

◊ ◊ ◊ ◊ ◊ ◊ ◊

The attacker has a gun instead of a knife. He's got the drop on you — you can't possibly draw and shoot before he shoots you, because action is always faster than reaction.

Now what?

Get out of the car and give him the keys. It's not worth your life.

◊ ◊ ◊ ◊ ◊ ◊ ◊

On a hot summer day, you're gassing up your car . . . too slowly for the customer behind you. He tells you to finish up and get out of his way. He turns off your pump and threatens you verbally.

Do you draw your gun?

No — unless he is showing a weapon or taking threatening action. Cap your tank. When you go inside to pay, tell the clerks what happened and ask them to call the police. If you take an unpleasant situation and turn it into a confrontation, you are backing the obnoxious person into a corner. If violence results, who is responsible? Think about it.

The point of all this is to show that no two confrontations are exactly alike. Human interactions tend to come in shades of gray more often than black and white. The old saying, "Discretion is the better part of valor," contains a lot of wisdom. Circumstances change even while you're in the process of making a judgment.

Many police officers reach the end of their careers without ever drawing — much less firing — a gun in line of duty. The odds against your ever needing to use your gun are even greater. But don't let this make you complacent. Be alert, be aware, and — as the Boy Scouts say — be prepared.

If you ever do have to use your gun in self-defense, go home and write yourself a letter. Describe everything that happened: what you saw, what you heard, what you did. Explain your feelings — fear? anger? — and any injuries you suffered. Note the names and addresses of witnesses. If you didn't get their names, figure out how to do it now. (e.g., Did they live or work near where the incident occurred?) Then ask these witnesses to write down what they remember, even if they've already given statements to the police. You can also request copies of these statements from the police.

The justice process moves slowly, and a year or so could easily go by before you will have to answer questions on the witness stand. Unless you write your recollections down when they are fresh, you may forget or confuse details. Your memory can be crucial to your legal position.

Part II: *More to Know*

After successfully completing a required CCW course, your curiosity may be aroused and you may want to learn more. Part II includes additional interesting and helpful information, but it is not part of most required courses. It is included here to reinforce and add to what you learned in Part I.

— 6 —
The Will to Survive

When children play Cops and Robbers, someone says, "Bang! Bang! You're Dead," and that's it. You have to fall down and give up. Get rid of that mindset. Once there's a bullet hole in *you,* you're justified in responding with whatever force is available. The attacker just tried to deprive your children of a parent and to widow your spouse.

Make up your mind to survive. The bad guys don't fight by the Marquis of Queensbury rules. They operate on a primal level, determined to get away from, around, or through you — and sometimes that lets them win when "the book" says they can't. You never know — on the street or in your home — what an aggressor will do next. Cover the threat with your gun for as long as it takes, until the aggressor flees or the police arrive and secure the scene.

Fools rush in

In police training, it's easy to set up a no-win scenario. I remember one in particular. I was supposed to be responding to a man-with-a-gun call, and no backup was available.

I had to traverse a long, lighted hallway to reach a staircase. No — I didn't think to unscrew the light bulb in the hall fixture, but I did a pretty good job of making my way from cover to cover down the hall. Finally, I came to the last good cover. Between me and the foot of that dark staircase stretched a good thirty feet of brightly lighted hallway — and it was dark at the top of those stairs. Isn't it always? Anyway, I paused to think it over, and the instructor spoke for the first time: "What are you going to do?"

"There's no way I can go any further with any certainty of survival," I said. "I'm going to back out and observe the scene until some backup arrives." In fact, that was exactly what the exercise was intended to teach: "Fools rush in where angels fear to tread." Backing off is not backing down, and there's no shame in being smart enough to avoid a losing fight.

That's what police officers are taught, so why would you rush inside to check your house if you came home and found the door ajar? Instead, go to a neighbor's house and call police. The situations you want to learn to handle are the ones you *can't avoid.*

Survival is really determined more by the mind than by the body. During one battle in World War II, a young lieutenant took one shot that neatly severed a very private part of his body. A grizzled sergeant took 13 hits from a machine gun. The lieutenant died. The sergeant recovered and lived a long, full life. The sergeant was a survivor, and survival is the only victory.

Determination counts

Sergeant Llew Rowe of the Connecticut State Police told me a frightening story. Working with an in-service class of young police officers, he gave a lecture on the physical and mental aspects of high-stress, violent encounters. In his talk, he emphasized both the importance of the will to survive and the role of perception in a life-threatening situation.

After the lecture, he took the group to the target range for practice and evaluation runs. At the seven-yard-line stage, one trainee suddenly screamed, "I'm hit! I'm hit!" and fell to the ground, clutching his leg. Range officers rushed to him and discovered that he had indeed been hit in the thigh by a bullet splatter. The injury amounted to no more than a slight cut. Of course, it must have stung and, coming so unexpectedly, scared the young man. But screaming and falling to the ground is no way to survive.

Let me assure you that this is not a matter of wanting the police officer to be *macho*. It is a question of wanting him or her to survive. When I tell this story in a training class, I follow with the story of a paintball exercise. The paintballs, of course, are not lethal, but they do sting. In this case, one trainee was playing the role of an officer who had the suspect covered. The "officer" was shielded by the corner of a building, but one of his legs was sticking out. The "suspect's" partner was able to hit the officer's thigh with a paintball. Reacting to the sting, the trainee reached over to grasp his leg — and was hit twice on his face shield. In real life, he would have been killed. So the rule is, *if you are hurt in a confrontation, address the threat first. Your injury can wait.*

The really lethal killers in a violent confrontation are indecision and confusion. Think about the situations in which you might find yourself. Try to decide in advance how you will handle them. Then, if the need arises, you'll be ready to act.

Consider this example from George Durkee of the National Park Service in California:

> We had an FBI instructor, and he showed us a film of a bank robbery. The robber is at the counter with a gun. Then, in the next few frames we see an officer enter the bank, carrying a shotgun in his right hand. There are a few people at the various counter windows, so the officer doesn't know which one is the robber or even whether an actual robbery is taking place.
>
> Anyway, as the officer comes around a big pillar, the robber turns and walks towards him. Then the film shows the robber's gun come up and puffs of smoke as he fires at the officer. He's only about three to five feet away. When the officer sees the

gun, he starts transferring the shotgun to his left hand to go for his revolver, but there's no way he can fire before the robber shoots him. The officer drops to floor, and the suspect runs out of bank.

Ironically, the officer wasn't actually hit. He must have figured that the robber couldn't miss at point blank range, so he *assumed* he was hit and went down.

We all tend to give up when we're "hit." Why? The police baton is considered a nonlethal weapon, but you could easily kill someone with it. The gun is considered lethal, but four out of every five persons shot by the police do not die.

Being shot by someone is clearly an offensive act, so by all means TAKE OFFENSE. You need to maintain self-control, but I can't think of anything better than genuine anger to focus your response to your attacker. Your injuries can provide that anger, but the injuries themselves are irrelevant as long as the threat remains. Your body can take a lot of punishment and still heal itself. What's more, it can continue to function in spite of the punishment. The lesson here is simple: *Never quit. Never give up.*

Little things mean a lot

The patrol physician for the South Carolina Highway Patrol, Dr. Carl Lopez, got an undergraduate degree in behavioral psychology. He verifies the police dictum that you will do in a fire fight what you've been taught on the practice range: "If your instructor in a role-playing scenario says, 'OK, you've been hit. Stop moving,' that's what you'll do in real life."

Unlike a lot of doctors, Dr. Lopez speaks in plain English. He explains that your physiological responses are not under your control (if you're sweating, you're sweating), but your psychological response *are*. And that psychological response can incapacitate you when it reaches your brain, your heart, or a major nerve center. On the other hand, it can signal the brain that something bad is happening and you need to respond. At that point, what you've been trained to do will take effect. Without training, you're likely to go for the primal response —curling up in a ball and protecting your head.

This is clearly no way to survive. But if you've had training, it will kick in at the signal from your brain. The stronger the signal, the stronger the trained response needs to be, and responses are strengthened by practice.

"Even very severe wounds may be counterbalanced by practice," Dr. Lopez says. "Physiological response sets a ceiling as to what you can accomplish. That ceiling is a lot higher than people realize."

Survival pyramid

The survival pyramid has three components: **skill**, **tactics**, and **equipment**. But it isn't a three-legged stool, with each leg of equal importance. **Skill** is the foundation. **Tactics** is the body of the structure. **Equipment** is the peak at the top.

> **Skill**: We can define this as proficiency or ability, but it's more than either of those. Before you can learn proper self-defense techniques, you must *want* to. Motivation is at the heart of your skills. That's why, when I teach, I no longer say, "*If* you are in a gunfight. . ." Now, I say, "*When* you are in a gunfight. . ." I want my students to master the necessary skills *and* to have confidence in their abilities.

> **Tactics**: Tactics are maneuvers, strategies for achieving a goal. They can be learned only by those who have mastered the necessary skills. If someone shoots at you, do you just stand there in the open and shoot back? Of course not. First you take cover. If you see a potential confrontation some distance away, you look for ways to avoid it.

> **Equipment**: Naturally, you need the best tools to do the best job. High capacity pistols let you carry more ammunition on your belt. Speedloaders are good for use with revolvers. But none of these will bring you safely through a violent encounter unless you have the skills to use them and have learned the tactics that will give you the best chance.

— 7 —
Serious Shooting for Self-defense

Why did you buy a handgun? I'll bet it's not because you want to take up target shooting. But how do you learn to use your costly new pistol or revolver? By going to the target range.

That's a fine idea, as far as it goes, but target practice can't teach you everything you need to know to become a competent *pistolero*. You need other kinds of training as well. You can't write the great American novel without learning that *i* comes before *e* except after *c* and that active verbs are stronger than passive ones. Mastery of the elementary aspects of any activity precedes work on advanced techniques.

Before you can fire your new handgun *reactively,* you must learn to shoot it on purpose. Note I did not say *instinctively.* You may have a natural talent for shooting, but the psychomotor skill of shooting (and hitting the target) is not instinctive. The muscular movement and the eye-hand coordination require practice. Even more practice is necessary to make this skill reactive — something you can do virtually without thinking about it. Instructors' estimates vary, but they generally concur that this takes between two thousand and four thousand repetitions. Think about when you learned to drive a car. At first, you had to consciously think "Move foot from accelerator to brake pedal" when you wanted to stop. After a while, you moved your foot without thinking. That's what I mean by *reactive.*

Much of your shooting skill lies in your mind: If you *believe* you can do it, you *can.* I recall the time I started a handgun course with a brand new S&W Model 66 with adjustable sights. I didn't have a chance to sight it in before I arrived for my class. The whole first day we worked on shooting from the hip, and I could barely keep my shots on target. After class, I adjusted the sights until they were dead-on, and the next day all my hip shooting shots hit smack in the middle of the paper. That sounds absurd — you don't even *use* the sights when you shoot from the hip. What the process of adjusting my gunsights did was give me confidence in the accuracy of my handgun.

Now, obviously, if you don't know/believe you can hit the target when you're shooting for practice, how can you believe you'll hit it under stress? Just observing improperly trained shooters will convince you that — just as you must know the ABCs before you write your novel — you must know the basic procedures before you can use your gun in self-defense.

Finding training

Many NRA pistol clubs and gun dealers around the country offer training in gun safety, stance, grip, master eye, sight alignment, sight picture, breath control, trigger control, and follow through. These courses are well worth your while. You can't learn to shoot by reading about it. Doing it under the instructor's watchful eye will help you avoid developing bad habits. Learn the fundamentals of marksmanship before you begin to train for serious shooting. You'll find many local clubs that teach target shooting, but fewer that teach practical shooting. If you ask around and do some research, though, you can probably find such training. Some clubs, for instance, train their members for IPSC matches.

Self practice

If you can't find formal instruction in practical shooting, you'll have to train yourself. Fortunately, this doesn't require the construction of an actual target range. A sandpit or old quarry with an embankment on three sides, in fact, is better than a range with only one backstop. Sharpen the feet of a target frame and you can stick it in the ground.

Let's assume then that you have a permit and that you wear your gun so that you can draw it quickly and smoothly. You've completed basic marksmanship training, and you have a safe place to practice shooting. You can draw your gun with one hand, aim, and hit the bull's-eye — or very close to it. Now you can begin to learn the practical techniques. I learned these in an advanced pistol course taught by Peter M. Tarley of Police Training Division, Inc., of Monsey, New York.

Think about *how* you're likely to be called on to use your gun. Police officers go into situations sensible citizens avoid, and the officers are trained to be prepared. Nevertheless, in 30 percent of some six thousand shooting incidents investigated by the New York City police, the need to shoot came as a surprise to the officers. For you — a civilian —showing your gun could be a crime in itself (that is, it could constitute a threat). It's a very good bet, therefore, that when you need to shoot, your gun will be in its holster.

So, your training begins with the gun in its holster and the retention strap snapped. The draw is best explained as a sequence of movements. (See the photographs in chapter 3.) Practice melding these movements into a single, smooth flow. Master smoothness before you try for speed. Speed will come naturally as the movements themselves become automatic and reflexive.

1. Grip the gun in the holster and use your thumb to unsnap the retaining strap. Remember to keep your finger *out of the trigger guard*. Meanwhile, bring your other hand forward about waist high.
2. Clear the gun from the holster — *finger still outside the trigger guard* — then straighten and lock your gun-hand wrist.
3. Push the gun forward, bringing your other hand up to meet it. Close your other hand over your gun-hand fingers for a two-hand grip.
4. Now the muzzle is safely past you, and you can slip your finger into the trigger guard.
5. Bring the gun to eye level, focus on the front sight. At short range, if the front sight is on the target the shot will hit home.

On TV, that's the end of it — but not in real life. Stay on target. Four out of five people who are shot do *not* drop over and die. The attacker may still come at you, even after three or four shots. If the attacker *is* stopped, lower the gun out of your line of sight (to break your tunnel vision), take your finger off the trigger, and scan left and right to see if anyone else might attack from a another direction. If you are certain there is no further threat, reholster the gun with one hand *without looking down.*

You may notice that, in all that description, there was no mention of your *stance.* If you draw your gun as indicated here, you'll naturally assume a stance similar to the one boxers use when they pose for photographs. The boxer holds his weak fist high in front for protection, keeping his stronger fist cocked close to his chest so he can throw a punch. Think about how you hold a rifle or shotgun, or a baseball bat. Your weak side is turned toward the threat and — in this case — your gun side is protected. This stance will probably come naturally to many athletes, but even if you aren't in that category, it'll become second nature with enough practice. Eventually, you'll be able to deliver a telling shot in the dark when you can't see your own gun or its sights.

That's the first exercise in developing reflexive shooting habits. Now find a safe place, unload your gun (be sure the magazine is empty and the chamber is clear), choose a spot to focus on as your target, and practice your draw. Before you draw, however, yell "Stop!" "Back off!" "Leave me alone!" "Don't make me use this!" or any other warning you can think of. If you do have to shoot, you can count on having to explain your actions in court. As your draw becomes smoother and begins to feel natural, practice shouting a warning *after* you draw and *before* you pull the trigger.

Again, bear in mind that you may shoot *only when you are threatened.* When the threat disappears, so does your justification for shooting. If you draw and your attacker comes to a screeching halt or turns and flees, you are no longer threatened and *you may not shoot.* So, although you want your actions to become reflexive, you also want to retain the option of reacting to changes in the situation. If the attacker comes at you again with a lead pipe in his hand, you're in position to do what you have to do. If he slinks away, you can spare yourself a very unpleasant experience.

Take as much time as you need to make your draw and your dry fire smooth and speedy. Practice getting a good sight picture when you bring the gun to eye level. At close range, however, seeing the front sight is more important than a precise sight alignment. Practicing point shooting will keep your focus on the threat — on your attacker.

Now it's time to go to the target range.

Self-taught exercises

The most dangerous thing in the world to anyone wearing a sidearm for serious business is an unloaded gun. Generations of target shooters grew up with these basic range rules:

1. Open the action.
2. Point it in a safe direction.
3. Be sure of your backstop.

The first rule on target ranges is *All guns must be unloaded except when they are in use on the firing line.* However, my rules of practical gun safety are:

1. The gun is always loaded.
2. Always point the muzzle in a safe direction.
3. Leave your finger off the trigger until you shoot.
4. Know what is beyond your target.

You carry the gun holstered on your hip and *loaded.* When you shoot it dry, reload. *Fast.*

If you wear a revolver, practice with speedloaders:

- Shift the gun to your weak hand as you open the cylinder.
- Dump the spent cases onto the ground with your weak-hand thumb and reach for a speedloader with your strong hand.

- Put the cartridges into the cylinder, release them, and drop the speedloader on the ground while your weak hand closes the cylinder.
- Grip the gun with your strong hand and bring it back into play.

If you use a semiautomatic, practice dropping the magazine as your weak hand reaches for a loaded spare on your weak side. Grab the magazine with the butt in the heel of your hand and your index finger pointing up the front of the magazine. That helps you steer it into the loading well without having to look away from the threat. Insert the fresh magazine so that it clicks into place, then thumb the slide release so that it puts a new cartridge into the chamber as it closes.

Sight alignment is all-important in basic target shooting, and you should include it in the early stages of your practical training. But, just as you eventually brake your car without thinking, you will learn to shoot without consciously sighting when speed is of the essence. When you drive your car, your brain actually does tell your foot to move from accelerator to brake, but it does this so rapidly that you are not conscious of the thought. Likewise, your brain gets a subconscious sight picture before it tells your trigger finger to pull. This sort of response comes only one way — from practice.

If the thought of shooting without careful sighting scares you, consider this: An analysis was made of 898 cases in which police officers were feloniously killed with firearms from 1975 to 1984. In 87 percent of those cases, the officers were within seven yards of their killers. At that distance, if you draw your gun properly and your front sight is on the target, your shot will hit — maybe not an absolute bull's-eye, but definitely in center of mass.

I emphasize the importance of draw and position, because I have great faith in "muscle memory." This type of memory comes from training one's mind. A place kicker looks at the ball as he kicks. A golfer looks at the ball as she swings. These athletes position themselves so that the ball will go between the goal posts or onto the green. Your muscle memory can direct the ball — or the bullet — to the right spot. A well-trained practical shooter can use a gun effectively even under adverse circumstances.

For your first shooting drill, set up a target; you can even use a blank piece of wrapping paper. In police training classes, we use realistic-looking targets, but it isn't necessary (in fact, a judge may wonder why you "practiced shooting people"). Stand about four yards from your target, and stand as you would if you were talking to the person (the target). Remember the boxer — weak side quartered forward, hands in front of your waist. Now *draw!* Look at your front sight, fire one shot, lower your gun slightly, and scan. Repeat this until you can consistently draw and hit the target somewhere in center mass in 2.25 seconds or less (from the point when your gun is concealed to the moment you shoot.) Don't forget to use your voice and get a challenge in there before you shoot.

Now go through this drill again, but draw and fire *two* quick shots. For this, you may need to educate your trigger finger. With a double action revolver, the trigger must go all the way forward — but your trigger finger should not lose contact with the trigger. If you're shooting a double action semiautomatic, the first shot is a loooong double action pull, but the second shot is single action. If you're accustomed to using a revolver, your trigger finger will travel halfway to Topeka before you fire that second shot. With a Glock, the trigger is a short-travel double action for every shot — always the same — but the action resets sooner so the trigger doesn't have to go all the way forward before you can shoot a second time.

At this point in your training, take the time with one-, two-, and three-shot drills in order to perfect your draw, tune your muscles to that telling first shot, and condition your trigger finger to keep contact with the trigger.

Watch it! You're trying for speed, aren't you? Speed is good, but for now the important things are smooth draw, prompt firing (as soon as your gun is at eye level), hitting with that first shot, and getting off a smooth second shot. That smoothness *must* come before speed. When you find yourself missing the target, going beyond your capability, slow down. Pete

Tarley says that if you slow down just .5 seconds, you'll start hitting again. Let your speed increase naturally. In that analysis of shooting incidents in which police officers were killed, the officer was alone, facing more than one assailant. That's important because it's likely that if you're accosted on the street you'll be up against more than one person. Both may have guns, or one will have a gun and the other a knife. Two may have knives and two others may have lead pipes or lengths of chain. That's why you should train yourself to deal with multiple targets.

Multiple adversaries

This introduces a new consideration into your training. How can you handle multiple adversaries?

This is why I prefer a sandpit to an actual shooting range. To practice facing more than one attacker, set up some targets at different heights and go through your two-shot drills, aiming one shot at each target. When you encounter more than one assailant, you should never try to hit each one twice. While you're "double-tapping" two, a third assailant can put a shot into you. That happened not long ago to a police officer in Texas. He's dead.

The officer was an avid IPSC shooter, in training for the national competition. He'd been repeating the El Presidente course which requires that each of three targets be double-tapped. After a practice session, he went on duty. The dispatcher sent him on an armed-robbery call at a liquor store. As he drove up to the store, three perpetrators came out with their guns blazing. The officer did what he'd been doing in practice, but as he was double-tapping his second "target," the third robber put a 32 slug into his neck.

These attackers don't necessarily cluster together either. They'll spread out, so set your targets with one in front, another to the left, and a third to the right. Of course, you need a backstop on three sides to do this exercise safely. If you have only a single backstop, spread the three targets as far apart as possible. It's a compromise, but it's better than not practicing these tactics at all. Unlike most targets, attackers don't stand still. In his classes, Pete Tarley used a portable moving-target rig with an overhead cable and electric motor that moved the target back and forth. Then he placed a shield in the middle, so the target would bob out from one side or the other or move twenty yards or so in either direction. Another instructor I know fills the hole of an old automobile tire with cardboard and rolls it across the range to give students practice with moving targets. And believe me, it's true that a moving target is harder to hit!

Defensive shooting means using cover. You can lean out to return fire while exposing as little of yourself as possible.

Think cover!

Once you're comfortable with these exercises, we move to your next concern: taking cover. When you are accosted by someone, it's unlikely that the two of you will be the only objects in the vicinity. CYA (Cover your . . . backside) is an applicable concept in any confrontation. Get something — a mailbox, a telephone pole, a fire hydrant, a dumpster, a parked car, even a curb if that's all the cover you can find — between you and the threat to your safety. If this cover will also deflect a bullet, that's even better. But any screen, even a thick bush, is likely to slow down your attackers. One instructor I know gave a student a dummy gun and told him to bring it up and pretend to shoot the instructor. But before the student could raise the gun, the instructor whipped out a newspaper and opened it in front of himself. The student all but turned himself inside out trying to get a clear shot. Why? (Which is what the instructor asked him.) Certainly, a bullet could penetrate the newspaper. But it's disconcerting to shoot at a target you can't see.

Once you recognize danger and it's clear you can't escape it, take cover and lean out to shoot if you need to.

— 8 —
What Makes a Hero?

All through this discussion of safe and responsible gun use, I've stressed the fact that you are legally justified in using your gun only to defend yourself or your loved ones from grievous bodily harm or death. But what if you stumble upon an attack on someone you don't even know?

I've said it's not your job to catch criminals, only to defend yourself, but what if . . .?

CompuServe has an online Police Forum. One day a man — we'll call him Fred — logged on to tell a story and ask a question. He'd been driving on a lonely road when he saw a woman motorist whose car was disabled. Another car had also pulled over, and a man was attacking the woman. Fred stopped. He was legally armed and he challenged the man, who appeared to be trying to rape the woman. When the attacker saw that Fred had a gun, he went back to his own car and left. But since that time Fred had wondered, "What would have happened if I'd shot him?"

Officers in the forum questioned Fred about various details, then assured him he had reacted properly to the situation. If the man had not backed away from the attack, Fred would have been justified in shooting him.

Stephene Ybarra of Dallas, Texas had a similar experience. He happened upon a young girl trying to fight off a man who was attacking her. He was unarmed, but he jumped out of his car and tackled the would-be rapist. He was strong enough to bring the man down and to hold him until the police arrived to take him into custody.

"It all happened on the spur of the moment," Ybarra says. "I thought it was just another day." But apparently not. In the next two weeks, Ybarra appeared on CNN and the *Today* show, received a citation from the city of Dallas, shook hands with the governor of Texas, and threw out the first ball at the Texas Rangers' opening day game. He shakes his head in perplexity when he hears the word "hero".

The issue of citizen intervention in crime has haunted the nation's collective conscience since 1964 when Kitty Genovese was stabbed to death on a New York City street while 38 people in nearby apartments watched the murder or heard her cries for help. None of those witnesses so much as called the police. They "didn't want to get involved."

Psychological studies

The Kitty Genovese case was the catalyst for many psychological studies, efforts to determine what characteristics were found in people who would go to the aid of a stranger in distress. Most results suggest that heroes are pretty much like everyone else.

Ted Huston, a professor of social psychology at the University of Texas at Austin, worked on such a study with Gilbert Geis, a professor of criminology at the University of California's Irvine campus. These two researchers were interested in the fact that behavior considered heroic in the United States is simply expected in other countries. In fact, in most places other than the United States or Great Britain, bystanders are *required by law* to come to the aid of a person under attack.

Huston and Geis studied sixty Californians who had intervened in violent crimes. They put these people through a battery of tests to discern characteristics, motivations, and thinking. The conclusions were clear and uncomplicated. Those who intervened were generally taller and heavier than the assailant they encountered (all but one of the interveners were male), and they believed they could prevail.

"They didn't do it because they wanted to be a hero," Huston says. "They felt they had stepped in because any decent citizen who is able should try to help."

Possible consequences

These good Samaritans were lucky. Several years ago in Dallas, a major-league umpire, Steve Palermo, tried to rescue two women from muggers. He was shot in the back, and paralyzed — but he never had second thoughts about his actions.

"The person who pulled that trigger is in prison for 75 years," reports Palermo, who still wears a brace on one leg and walks with a cane. "We're all responsible for the consequences of our actions." To have any regrets, he contends, "would trivialize the lives of the two women and say they weren't worth it. What I did wasn't chivalrous and it wasn't macho. It was the right thing to do." According to Penn State psychologist Lance Shotland, another researcher into bystander intervention, Palermo fits the typical profile. Steve was with four other people, so they outnumbered the muggers and they were working together. The situation was unambiguous: There was no doubt that the two women needed help. The appearance of the gun was unexpected. Bystanders rarely intervene when they see the assailant is armed.

Shotland has found that "People are less likely to help when they're among strangers. When they're with friends, they can communicate and work out a plan of action. Even then, if the situation is ambiguous . . . people begin to tell themselves that it isn't really that serious."

Shotland conducted one study by staging attacks around unsuspecting bystanders. A man would appear to be beating a woman. When the woman screamed, "Get away! I don't know you!" the bystanders would intervene. When she screamed, "Get away! I don't know why I married you!" most did not help.

What, if anything, does all this have to do with your training for a carry permit or learning safe and responsible use of a firearm? Well, in Part I we addressed questions of self-defense and defense of your loved ones. But, as a good citizen, if you are legally armed and you come upon a violent crime in which you can help the victim, you don't want to turn away and let someone be murdered. Nevertheless, you should be aware of the possible consequences: you could be a hero, but you could also be paralyzed or dead.

— 9 —
Training Is All in Your Mind

There is not, and there never will be, enough time for training. You can expand your time, however, if you repeat physical exercises in your imagination. How much time do you spend waiting in line? On hold? Showering and brushing your teeth. Use these opportunities. Imaginary practice can do nearly as much good as the actual exercises.

"Research finds that imagining the movements stimulates the same areas of the brain — except for the motor cortex — as physical practice does," says Roland Ouellette, director of R.E.B. Training International of Stoddard, New Hampshire. "Under stress, the body responds automatically to instilled habits. Mental conditioning puts data into your long-term memory. Mental practice is effective because it is these memories that control your muscles."

So the excuse that you have no time to practice is no excuse at all.

"I can do a whole specific program in my head in two minutes," Ouellette says. "I can visualize myself doing all the techniques in confronting an aggressor. The more I practice mentally, the more automatic my response becomes."

Mind games

The Harding-Kerrigan affair was a virtual mind game. Nancy Kerrigan's coach made a major issue of the fact that Nancy and Tonya had to practice in the same place and at the same time. He said it put his skater under psychological stress. Competitors from other countries, he contended, would not suffer this stress because they had not been victimized by Harding. Actually, it could be argued that skating under stress would *prepare* Nancy for the stress of Olympic competition.

This is a little like the realistic simulation that is part of police baton training. In these exercises, the trainees wear protective garb so that they can actually strike one another with the baton as they might strike a belligerent drunk in real life. Without such protective gear, the trainees would have to fake a blow with the baton and they would never learn how to deliver a forceful blow. Their minds would be conditioned to stopping short. When I referred to "muscle memory" in the context of firearms training, I was using an inaccurate term. Your muscles have no memory — but your brain does. Repetitive practice of anything from shooting to golfing to playing the piano is actually exercising the brain. So mental exercise can be as beneficial as the physical version

I used to think of "mental conditioning" in terms of being alert and decisive and reacting promptly in a threatening situation. But it's more than that. To gain the advantage of surprise as you execute any defensive technique, you must act quickly. Speed is essential, and speed in thinking comes first. You can't stop to wonder whether the aggressor really means to swing that lead pipe at you. Quick thinking is at least as important as quick hands and feet. Action has no purpose unless a proper reaction has been practiced so that it becomes reflexive.

The desire to learn determines one's capacity to learn. If you take a pistol permit class simply because it's required before you can get a permit, you won't get much out of it. If you take it so that you can defend yourself and your family, you will benefit far more.

Mental exercises

See that little old lady coming toward you? What if she were to swing her umbrella at your head? Try to imagine how you would ward off her blow.

See the dark corner ahead? What if someone leaps out with a gun in his hand? Would you draw and shoot? Dive for cover? What cover?

If you can picture yourself going through the motions as you react to these and other imagined incidents, you will improve your ability to respond quickly. There's no substitute for good, hard, comprehensive physical practice — but there's also no substitute for mental conditioning. For one thing, if you practice as you walk down the street, it will keep you alert.

There's one factor in an actual confrontation that you can't simulate in practice: *fear*. Real brawls aren't logical and don't follow a pattern of give-and-take the way fights on television do. The real thing is a flurry of blows and screams and kicks and shoves. If you can imagine a real-life fight, you will be better prepared when one erupts in your vicinity.

— 10 —
Defending Yourself in Court

In New Haven, Connecticut, an attorney for an offender's family brought an excessive force suit against local police officers who had shot and killed the aggressor in what was eventually determined to be a "good shoot." In the course of their confrontation, the officer had double-tapped the offender. The autopsy showed the officer's first bullet was fatal, so the second shot was unnecessary and must therefore constitute excessive force.

In a similar case, an 18-year-old, high on crack, attacked some people with a broom handle. He threatened the police officer who intervened, and the officer fired multiple shots from his 17-round magazine before the threat was ended. The boy's family sued on the grounds of excessive force.

These cases — typical of most such lawsuits — were not successful. I continue to teach people to double-tap. The answer to the question, "How many shots should I fire?" is still "Shoot until the threat is ended." After all, the only reason you fire your gun is *to stop the aggressor's felonious assault.*

Dr. Carl Lopez has strong opinions about these legal actions. "I've had the experience of pronouncing people dead at least a dozen times in my career," he says. "The procedure consists of trying to get a verbal response, checking the pupillary response in the eyes, listening for heart and breath sounds, checking for pulse, checking for a pain response . . . and then repeating the sequence a few seconds later. In my professional opinion, taking such steps while trying to protect oneself from a still-moving perpetrator who is capable of exerting deadly force is tantamount to suicide."

Survival on the street and in court

You are trained to double-tap an aggressive target because, very often, one bullet from a handgun will *not* stop an assault. If two shots don't stop it, keep shooting. One instructor answers the question of "How many times?" with "Keep shooting as long as the target is in your sights."

So that will help you survive on the street. What about in court?

Your training program is your first defense: "Your honor, I did what I've been trained to do." This, of course, shifts the burden to your instructor, so instructors should be careful to document their reasons for this aspect of the training — and for all other aspects as well. They may have to justify this training in court. The second defense refers to Dr. Lopez's remarks: "Your honor, I am not qualified to determine whether someone is dead and is no longer a threat to me. All I could do was respond to the threat I perceived at the time, and I stopped shooting when I believed that the threat was ended."

Written reports

Remember that we advised you to write down a full description of any shooting situation in which you are involved. Years may go by before an aggressor's family brings its "wrongful death" suit to court. After a shooting, you may be traumatized and eager to forget the experience as quickly as possible. If you haven't written it down, what will happen to you on the witness stand when you are questioned about every detail?

It may help to use the format newspaper reporters are taught: include Who, What, Where, When, Why, and How:

Who: Everyone — participants, witnesses, victims, and police officers.

What: The situation as you observed it, noting the words and actions of all the *Whos* and your own feelings — including the reasons you believed you were in mortal danger.

When: Specific times — as best you can pinpoint them — and the sequence of events.

Where: Specific location of the incident, including any change of scene.

Why: The motive — if you know it — of a criminal act (robbery, rape, revenge) and your reasons for responding as you did.

How: The way a situation developed and how you made your decision to respond.

What incidents should be written down? Any situation in which you played a part. A written record will enable you to explain your actions and to recall details.

The ABCs of report writing are *Accuracy, Brevity, Clarity, and Completeness.*

It's also important that you write your report in good, correct English. Look at this example:

> The driver tossed a gun to the passenger. He opened his door and took aim at me. I fired and he dropped. I covered the driver and ordered him to lie spread-eagled on the ground. The passenger appeared to be dead and I gained control of the situation.

Notice the early ambiguities here, surrounding the pronoun "he." Who took aim? The driver or the passenger? Did the driver drop when he saw your gun? Did the passenger drop because he was hit? Quoted out of context by a lawyer, these statements make it seem that your recollections are unclear.

Your response to a violent threat may be an unquestionably "good shoot," and you may have had the soundest possible basis for your decision to fire your gun. Be sure you have everything to support these facts when you go into court, no matter how much time has elapsed.

A lawyer's warning

My good friend Walt MacDonald has seen the problems created by improper or incomplete reports from both sides of the bar. Walt is the captain in charge of tactical operations and narcotics for the Plymouth County, Massachusetts, Sheriff's Department. He is also a practicing attorney, who says the importance of a written report cannot be overemphasized.

When you bring your report into court, the opposing attorney is provided with a copy. Whether you have been called as a prosecution witness (in the case against your assailant), a civil defendant (in a wrongful-death suit brought by the family of the person you shot), or a criminal defendant (if you are charged with an unjustified use of force), you will be subject to cross-examination based on your report. Your report will be compared to your sworn testimony, and what *isn't* in the report may be as significant as what *is*. You will almost certainly be asked some form of this question: "Is your memory of these events clearer today than it was immediately after the incident?" Any facts and details mentioned on the witness stand but omitted from the report may be rejected as "recent contrivances." The opposing attorney will argue that your testimony should coincide with your report. "If it's not in your report, it didn't happen," MacDonald says. Be absolutely certain that *everything* is in your report.

Recommended Reading

I hope this book, in addition to teaching the fundamentals of gun ownership, will spark your curiosity about guns and the many challenging sports that involve guns. With that in mind, I offer a list of suggested readings:

In the Gravest Extreme: The Role of Firearms in Personal Protection [ISBN 0-936279-00-1] by Massad Ayoob.

This book is acclaimed by police officers, judges, and lawyers (who report that they learned more about self-defense law from this book than they did in law school). Anti-gunners call it, "a guide on how to kill criminals and get away with it," but Lt. Frank McGee, former head of firearms training for the New York City Police Department, says it's "must reading" for anyone who keeps a gun for self-defense.

[Available at $9.95, plus $3.95 s&h, from Police Bookshelf, P.O. Box 122, Concord, NH 03302-0122. Phone orders: (800) 624-9049. Customer service: (603) 224-6814. Fax: (603) 226-3554. Email: 74767.370@compuserve.com]

CCW: Carrying Concealed Weapons — How to Carry Concealed Weapons and Know When Others Are [ISBN 0-941540-24-3] by Jerry Ahern.

This is the definitive book on choosing weapons —not only guns. It tells you where on your body you should position the gun, how to spot someone else who is armed, and how to choose the right holster for your gun. Ahern even explains how holsters are made. He thoroughly covers subjects on which *The Practical Pistol Manual* only touches.

[$14.95, plus $3.00 s&h, from Blacksmith Corp., 830 North Road #1 East, Chino Valley, AZ 86323. Phone orders:

(800) 531-2655, or (520) 636-4456. Fax: (520) 636-4457.
Email: bcbooks@northlink.com]

Armed & Female [ISBN 0-312-92332-5] by Paxton Quigley.
Quigley served on Senator Ted Kennedy's (D-Mass.) staff, was a member of the National Committee for Handgun Control, and helped pass the Gun Control Act of 1968. She's an intelligent woman — and when GCA-68 didn't reduce crime as its proponents had promised it would, she wanted to know why. And she did some homework. Today, she's a handgun expert, a competition shooter, and a security consultant. She has also worked as a bodyguard for several executives and celebrities. Her unique perspective, intensive research, and thorough treatment of issues make this book "must" reading for any female who is thinking about arming herself.
[$5.99, available from St. Martin's Paperbacks, 175 Fifth Avenue, New York, NY 10010.]

The Seven Steps to Personal Safety [ISBN 1-883663-01-X] by Richard B. Isaacs and Tim Powers.
This book tells you how to avoid a violent confrontation, how to deal with it if it's unavoidable, and how to survive its aftermath. It goes deeply into precautions and avoidance strategies, stressing awareness of your environment, ways to create distance between yourself and an adversary, and handling the violent incident itself. Personal defense aerosol sprays are discussed.
[$14.95 from The Center for Personal Defense Studies, P.O. Box 1225, Brookline, MA 02146-0010.]

Stopping Power [ISBN 1-882639-03-0] by J. Neil Schulman.
Schulman explains why seventy million Americans own guns. An award-winning novelist, this author became fed up with the media's focus on anti-gun arguments and their corresponding neglect of cases in which guns saved lives. He says, "I wrote *Stopping Power* to set the record straight and to prove that without private gun ownership, we'd all be less safe and even more violent, and our politics would be run by outright gangsters."

[$22.95 ($29.95 in Canada) from Synapse-Centurion, 225 Santa Monica Blvd. #1204, Santa Monica, CA 90401. Phone orders: (310) 829-2752.]

Realistic Defensive Tactics [ISBN 0-935878025] by John Peters.

Developed by the founder of the Defensive Tactics Institute, this is an illustrated guide to the proper use of a number of proven self-defense techniques. [$17.95]

Women's Views on Guns and Self-Defense, edited by William Garrison, Jr.

Provides a shocking view of today's reality. Compiles 15 papers, most written by women, that reveal some of the less pleasant reasons women own guns. [$5.50]

Effective Defense: The Woman, The Plan, The Gun [ISBN 1-885036019] by Gila May-Hayes.

A complete handbook of personal defense for women in the '90s. May-Hayes shares her knowledge in this well-written manual. [$13.95]

Not an Easy Target [ISBN 0-67189-081-6] by Paxton Quigley.

Gives you knowledge and strength to avoid personal attacks and to fight back when trouble strikes. Whether it's carjackings, rape, robbery, or domestic violence, Quigley offers a sensible approach for women. [$11.00]

To Keep and Bear Arms [ISBN 0-6474893-069] by Joyce Lee Malcolm.

Illuminates the historical facts underlying the current debate about gun-related violence and the Brady Bill. This book explains how this American right was carved directly out of English common law. Hardcover [$32.95].

The Truth About Self-Protection [ISBN 0-317644521] by Massad Ayoob.

A comprehensive guide for those interested in keeping themselves and their families secure. Ayoob blends his extensive research as a police officer into one compendium of information. [$7.99]

[The preceding six books are also available from Second Amendment Foundation, 12500 NE Tenth Place, Bellevue WA 98005. Phone orders (206) 454-7012.]

SAFE, NOT SORRY: Keeping Yourself and Your Family Safe in a Violent Age, by Tanya K. Metaksa, is a comprehensive, easy-to-follow guide to teach women how to provide their own protection. Based on the NRA's Refuse to Be a Victim program, it shows you how to rate your personal vulnerability and suggests steps to improve your safety and your family's security.
[Available from Harper Collins Publishing, 10 E. 53rd St. New York, NY 10022-5244. Phone: (212) 207-7000, Fax: (212) 207-7901. ISBN 006039191X. Hardcover ($23.00)].

Pepper Sprays for Self-defense
This video features two leading trainers, Ed Nowicki and Roland Ouellette, who demonstrate how oleoresin capsicum (OC) aerosol sprays are most effectively employed. OC provides a self-defense alternative in situations which would not justify the use of deadly force.
[$29.95 from Performance Dimensions, Inc., P.O. Box 502, Powers Lake, WI 53159-0502. Phone orders: (800) 877-7413. Customer service: (414) 279-3850. Fax: (414) 279-5758. 17 minutes.]

There are hundreds of books addressing virtually every specific concern or interest related to guns —from history to collecting to Olympic competition. If your interest is in issues of gun legislation, look for *Restricting Handguns: The Liberal Skeptic Speaks Out* [ISBN 0-88427-034-3], edited by Don G. Kates, Jr. This is the definitive treatise on the subject.

About the Author

Bill Clede is a former police officer and long-time freelance writer. He is technical editor of LAW and ORDER magazine and a correspondent for Washington Crime News Service. He is the author of *Police Officer's Guide, Security Officer's Manual, Police Handgun Manual, Police Shotgun Manual,* and *Police Nonlethal Force Manual.* He conducted his first police pistol class in the late 1940s and has been a certified firearms instructor ever since. He is a charter member of the International Association of Law Enforcement Firearms Instructors and a member of the American Society of Law Enforcement Trainers.